If Your Child Is Bipolar

The Parent-to-Parent Guide to Living with and Loving a Bipolar Child

Cindy Singer
Sheryl Gurrentz

PERSPECTIVE
PUBLISHING

LOS ANGELES

D0661580

Published by Perspective Publishing, Inc.
2528 Sleepy Hollow Dr. #A, Glendale, CA 91206
800-330-5851; 818-502-1270; fax: 818-502-1272
books@familyhelp.com
www.familyhelp.com

Additional copies of this book may be ordered by calling toll
free 1-800-330-5851, or by sending $22.95 ($18.95 + $4 shipping) to the
above address. CA residents add 8.25% ($1.56) sales tax. Discounts
available for quantity orders. Bookstores, please call Independent
Publishers Group (IPG) at 800-888-4741.

Library of Congress Cataloging-in-Publication Data

Singer, Cindy, 1965-
  If your child is bipolar : the parent-to parent guide to living with
and loving a bipolar child / Cindy Singer, Sheryl Gurrentz.
      p. cm.
  ISBN 1-930085-06-0 (pbk.)
  1. Manic-depressive illness in children--Popular works. I. Gurrentz,
Sheryl, 1965- II. Title.
  RJ506.D4S565 2003
  618.92'895--dc22

                                                          2003015655

Cover Illustration by Sam Ustun
Interior Illustrations by Julia Ustun and Joseph Gurrentz
Back Cover Photo by Jeff Sanders
Printed in the United States of America
First Edition

Dedication

♥   *For Julie: My beautiful daughter and the light of my life. I am so proud of the incredible young woman you have become. I have grown and learned so much from you. I am a better person every day that I have the privilege of being your mother. You are the best part of every day…I love you infinity plus one.* (Cindy)

For Jesse: my brother, my friend. It's a good thing you can read my mind because I can't find strong enough words to describe how incredibly special you are to me. I am so thankful that you still are and always will be part of my life. (Sheryl)

We admire your strength, bravery and dedication to making the most of your lives with Bipolar Disorder. Our deepest gratitude for so willingly serving as Exhibit A and Exhibit B for this book, describing your most difficult thoughts so we could try to understand how children with Bipolar Disorder think and feel, and allowing us to share so many personal aspects of your lives. You've not only done an incredible job of overcoming the difficulties in your lives, but now your experiences will help others who are following in your footsteps.

And, this is for all the children and adults who have gone undiagnosed or untreated and lost their lives as a result of the symptoms of this disorder. In honor of your memory and your interrupted lives, may this book prevent even one more person from sharing your fate.

Acknowledgements

Writing a book, like treating Bipolar Disorder, takes a lot of support and a strong team. Thank you to our family and friends, who were so supportive of the time and energy it took to write this book and shared their own experiences of living with and loving a child with a mental disorder. Many thanks go to Gwen Smith, who generously shared her extensive professional knowledge of pediatric psychopharmacology and guided us through the intricacies of dealing with pharmacists and medications. Our thanks also go to the many, many parents who shared their experiences, challenges and parenting solutions. And finally, we thank the many mental healthcare professionals who treated our family members with respect and helped them find the right combination of medications and therapy to help them live happier, more stable lives.

♥   In addition, Cindy gratefully acknowledges:

The best mother, father and sister in the world: I am so incredibly fortunate to have you in my life. You are my constants, my role models, my friends, and my backbone. I can't imagine my life without you. I love you so much.

My friend and co-author Sheryl Gurrentz: Thank you for always being only a phone call away. Thank you for laughing with me, crying with me, learning with me, worrying with me, and celebrating with me through it all. Thank you for loving and supporting me even when I was distant and so involved in my own life that I wasn't much of a friend in return. Thank you for helping me put all my jumbled emotions, experiences, and information into this manuscript that I am so proud of. But most of all, thank you for loving Julie and Sam so unconditionally. I love and admire you so much.

Molly Conahan, Caryn Ginsburg, Michelle Stark, Linda Levy, and Gwen Smith: Thank you for being the most wonderful friends a girl could ever have. Your support, encouragement, understanding, and love have nourished me through the darkest days of my life and made the best days of my life that much sweeter.

Betty and Semih: You believed in me and encouraged me when I decided I wanted to write this book. Thank you for making me feel valued and appreciated as the mother of your grandchildren and for never judging me or making me feel unsupported in the many difficult decisions I have made over the years for my children. I hope that this book will be part of a healing process for us all.

I would also like to offer my deepest appreciation to Dr. Lisa Renner. You have spent countless hours striving toward Julie's wellness and quality of life. She is here and well because of your expertise and tireless effort. Words are quite inadequate to express the level at which you have touched the lives of my family.

Table of Contents

Introduction
♥ Cindy's Story

I still remember the day I found out I was pregnant with Julie. The hopes and dreams for my life and my baby were not totally clear, but they were incredibly exciting. I can even remember exactly what I was wearing and the eerie feeling of not being alone in my own skin. After trying to get pregnant for over six months, we were ecstatic. We took a big bouquet of pink and blue balloons to my parents' house to tell them the exciting news.

That was twelve years ago. Things turned out very differently than I had imagined. I feel as if I have so many experiences to share: wonderful ones, terrifying ones, and everything in between. I have felt so alone for so long. Even though I have an incredible support system of family and friends, the emotional burden I carry can be suffocating.

When Julie was diagnosed with Bipolar Disorder at age six, I went on a mission to educate myself, to give myself some sort of control over this monster that was invading my child's mind, body and soul. Unfortunately, I found no information that applied to young children. I read all I could about teens and adults and tried to make it applicable to her. I have felt my way through the darkness, trying desperately to learn as I go and make as few mistakes as possible.

Approximately two million people in this country have been diagnosed with Bipolar Disorder. We can't even begin to count the number of people who have no diagnosis or an incorrect one, or the number of people who have taken their lives as a result of this illness. I truly believe what recent research is finding: although the average age of diagnosis is 28, the onset of symptoms for some people begins much, much earlier . . . even as early as infancy. Some moms even think their children's activity in utero was manic! I am extremely lucky to have gotten a diagnosis for my daughter at such a young age. I am hopeful that this will make a difference in her long-term prognosis.

I am a completely different person and parent from the place where I started. I feel as if I have traveled a very long way down a very dark path. Emotionally and intellectually, I have changed and grown. Unfortunately, most of this change came about from trial and error. I tend to be a "fixer" of problems. In this case, however, there was no "how-to" manual with step 1, 2, and 3 to follow to get from point A to point B. So, after years of mistakes, successes, and everything in between, I have learned many things. I would like to share some of the things that I wish desperately I had known much sooner.

If Your Child is Bipolar provides practical information to help you acknowledge and deal with your feelings about having a child whose behavioral and mood difficulties might be a sign of a mental disorder. It will help you face the challenge of going through the diagnostic process and understand what it means to get a diagnosis of Bipolar Disorder or another mental illness. It will also teach you how to manage the realities of your life in order to lessen the negative effects these types of disorders, and in particular Bipolar Disorder, can have on you, your child, and your family. It focuses on learning to understand and love the child you really have and appreciating and accepting the life you are living. Most importantly, it offers support and encouragement that will help you feel less alone. Other resources can help you with the more medical and clinical aspects of helping your child. This book is intended to empower and nourish you so that you can be the best parent you can be and take care of your own emotions and needs at the same time.

This book is my way of turning what has been unequivocally the biggest challenge in my life into something tangibly positive, something that I hope will pave a smoother path for someone else along their journey of living with and loving a Bipolar child.

Note from the authors:

If your child is Bipolar, you will find a great deal of information, suggestions, and stories in this book that specifically address living with and loving a Bipolar child. However, while the emphasis of this book is Bipolar Disorder, you might not know right now whether or not your child has a mental disorder, let alone Bipolar Disorder. So, you'll find that the first few chapters guide you through the process of evaluating whether or not mental illness seems like a realistic cause of your child's difficulties. This process is the same regardless of the type of mental disorder that is diagnosed. This information is not intended to help you diagnosis your child. Instead, it will help you do what you need to do to help your child. It will also help you handle the difficult emotions that arise when you admit to yourself and others that your child may have difficulties that can't be addressed with different parenting techniques, a special diet, or a new school. The suggestions about finding and interacting with the right professionals for your child's healthcare team, dealing with medicating your child, taking care of yourself and other family members while you care for your difficult child, and planning for the future apply no matter what type of diagnosis is made. And, since many children who are eventually diagnosed with Bipolar Disorder are first diagnosed with other disorders, it can only be helpful to be aware of other parents' experiences as you weave your way through the complexities of parenting this very special child.

Both Cindy and Sheryl have first-hand experience with having a Bipolar child in the family. Cindy's descriptions of her life as Julie's mother are marked with a ♥ throughout the book. Numerous other parents, as well as Julie's father and Cindy's family and friends share stories as well. Even though some of the names have been changed, the stories are real. They reflect the experiences of families living with and loving a Bipolar child.

Sheryl's descriptions of watching her brother Jesse, her parents, Cindy, and Julie deal with Bipolar Disorder are provided in certain sections to provide the perspective of a sibling of a Bipolar child, a friend of the parent of a Bipolar child, and a member of a family affected by Bipolar Disorder. Sheryl's personal stories reflect the experiences of a family living with and loving an adult whose childhood-onset Bipolar Disorder was not diagnosed or treated until he was in his late twenties.

We hope these stories help you see the experiences of families dealing with childhood-onset Bipolar Disorder through both experienced and objective eyes, realize the importance of diagnosing and treating the disorder as early as possible, and learn how friends and other family members feel about and relate to the experience. We also hope these stories help people who care about the parent of a Bipolar child acknowledge their own feelings and provide as much support and understanding as possible.

SECTION ONE:

Figuring Out What You're Dealing With

1
What is Wrong with My Child?

A baby is born. A tiny, precious bundle of all your hopes and dreams for the future. At some point, all parents find out that reality doesn't match up perfectly with fantasy, but for some parents, the difference is drastic.

Your child's behavior may make your parenting experiences feel like a nightmare. To say that you have a "difficult child" may not cut it. You may feel helpless to control your child's behavior. Nothing seems to work; yet you keep trying. It seems like you understand your child better than anyone else, but what you do know isn't nearly enough. You don't know what to do next.

Well, . . . you are not alone. Millions of parents have been at this same point, too. They now realize that changing parenting strategies, schools, playmates, or diet isn't enough.

It's time to ask, "Is there something wrong with my child?"

♥   *When your child cries inconsolably for hours on end, attacks you with a fork, tries to trip you down the stairs or kicks, hits, and spits at you on a daily basis like Julie did, you can't help but wonder if something is wrong.*

Is This You?

If many of the following descriptions characterize your life as a parent, you're probably right to think that what you're dealing with is beyond the scope of "normal," even for a difficult child.

▲ Your everyday life seems different and much more difficult than that of your friends with children the same age.

▲ Daily routines that should be easy are almost always a struggle.

▲ You own shelves full of parenting books with techniques that are ineffective for your child.

▲ You use all the same parenting techniques your friends use. They succeed while you fail.

▲ Your child's problem behaviors may be similar to those of other children, but they are more intense, last longer, and are harder or impossible to control.

▲ You feel like your family life is out of control. Your child's moods and behaviors dictate family activities and control the atmosphere of your home.

▲ People comment on how bright your child is, but you'd gladly deduct 20 points from her IQ if it would make life easier for both of you.

▲ Intellectually you know you are a good parent, but you are beginning to feel like a failure.

▲ You think it's possible that something may really be wrong with your child.

▲ Your child's behavior is at its worst when he's with you.

▲ Your child is fine all day at school, but the minute she sees you, she falls apart.

▲ You're nervous about sending your child to friends' homes because his behavior is so unpredictable.

CINDY'S STORY

♥ *When Julie was a baby, she cried all the time. It was as if she were in unbearable pain. Jeff and I took turns holding and rocking her almost all of her waking hours. I don't think we ate a meal together for a year. One night in a state of total exhaustion and confusion because she was crying so hard, I started to sob and yell at Jeff, "What is wrong with her? I know something is wrong with her!"*

Colic, the doctors told us, but in my heart I knew it was much more than that. Julie was like a tremendous force trapped inside a little body. She wanted to be held all the time, but she was so stiff. She would never relax and conform to my body. Instead she would arch her back and push away. From the time she could hold her head up, she resisted resting her head on my shoulder. Her head would be bobbing from exhaustion before she would lay it down to sleep. She seemed angry and frustrated most of the time. Surprisingly, she was at her best at parties. She loved the commotion. I always said that she would be a really well behaved child if we could provide a three-ring circus 24 hours a day.

I counted the days before each "well-check" appointment. I thought for sure I would get some answers, but each time they told me she was perfectly healthy. I dreaded the end of the appointment when the doctor would leave the room and I realized that I was once again going home without knowing what to do. I wanted to scream at him to please not leave me alone with her, to please not send me home again to face the endless hours of crying and sleepless nights. Instead, I was silent. But the pediatrician knew. He looked at me, shook his head, and said, "You will be butting heads with her your entire life, but I promise one day she will make you very proud." At the time this meant nothing to me; now it is my promise for the future.

A full night's sleep didn't happen for fifteen months. I cannot begin to describe the loneliness of all those dark nights—up all alone, trying desperately night after night to console her, to get her to sleep. I remember some nights sobbing along with her, thinking to myself that I had ruined my life and that I must be a terrible mother. There were many times I thought I was losing my mind. I remember one night I was afraid to walk near the banister because I thought I might not be able to control an urge to throw her over the side. I know there have been times that I've walked the line of madness.

Julie reached all her developmental milestones early, physical as well as intellectual. She walked at 8 1/2 months and talked in full sentences by her second birthday. Her frustration level did seem to subside a bit with each major milestone, but it usually didn't last long.

Severe tantrums became a part of normal life. The tantrums were usually daily, sometimes multiple times per day, and lasted one to two hours at a time. I couldn't believe that she could scream so loud, for so long. She was entirely out of control and would try to hit and kick me. I would hold her from behind in a kind of backwards hug with my legs holding her legs and my arms holding her arms, restraining her until she stopped only out of sheer exhaustion. Sometimes I would have to hold her head as well to keep her from biting me. The most confusing part was that a seemingly unimportant occurrence or a minor inconvenience usually instigated the tantrum. A simple "no" would trigger a tantrum that would ruin an entire day.

It was obvious from early on that Julie was very bright. Virtually everyone who came in contact with her would comment on her intelligence and verbal skills. She was the most articulate, precocious child I had ever seen. I began to attribute her difficulties to her giftedness, which was a much easier pill to swallow than any of the other possibilities that were starting to swirl around in my mind. I felt that her irritability must stem from the frustration of her body not being able to keep up with her brain. Even so, I never felt pride when other mothers would comment on how smart Julie was. I felt envy. Their children were "normal" and happy—my child was a complicated puzzle that I couldn't solve. I knew that she wasn't happy and carefree like other children. I still to this day cannot be sure that I consider giftedness a gift. It is a tremendous challenge and yet another way that my child is different. What's more, once we put Julie in a school for gifted children, it became clear that giftedness was not the problem. She continued to have severe behavior problems.

By the time Julie was five I was certain that either something was wrong with her beyond being just a "difficult" child or there was something terribly wrong with me as a parent. I read every parenting book I could find. Nothing seemed to work for Julie. I filled my bookshelves with The Difficult Child, The Challenging Child, The Out-of-Sync Child, The Underachieving Child, Helping Your Depressed Child, The Explosive Child, Parenting with Love and Logic, 1,2,3 Magic, Parent Effectiveness Training. *I took parenting classes. I bought special music, games and workbooks for children with anger management problems, oppositionality, empathy problems, attentional issues. The approaches in the books seemed to make sense, but none of them worked for any length of time. The problem was that there was no logic to her behavior. She was so irritable and oppositional and no amount of reinforcers, time-outs, points, stars, etc. were going to motivate her to change her behavior because she was not capable of changing her behavior. I was beginning to realize that my attempts to "fix it" might not work.*

Eventually we had to put a lock on the outside of her bedroom door so she could be kept safe and separate from us when she was out of control. I think this was one of the hardest things we ever had to do. Even now, after numerous doctors, therapists, and other parents have told us it was the right thing to do, I still feel a wave of nausea at the thought. Intellectually, I know it was the right thing. I had to protect her from hurting herself as well as from hurting others. A person without a child like this can never imagine what it is like to listen to your child behind a closed door making sounds like a crazed animal and not knowing how to help her.

THE POSSIBILITY OF A NEURODEVELOPMENTAL DISORDER

If you've read this far, chances are that your concerns about your child's behavior are well-founded. Like millions of other children, your child may have behavior problems that are symptomatic of a neurodevelopmental disorder. It may be hard to think about this possibility, especially because there is so much stigma attached to any term even remotely implying "mental illness."

There are many terms that are currently used to refer to these types of disorders. For the most part, they are interchangeable and will be used that way in the text of this book. You may want to choose the one that feels the most comfortable and substitute it for any others that may not feel right to you. Some examples of these terms are:

▲ Mental illness

▲ Mental disorder

▲ Neurodevelopmental disorder

▲ Neurobiological disorder

▲ Neuropsychological disorder

▲ Psychodevelopmental disorder

▲ Brain disorder

▲ Behavioral disorder

▲ Mood disorder

Regardless of what you call it, these disorders are no different than other types of health disorders except that their symptoms involve a person's behavior as opposed to a particular body part. Nevertheless, people tend to misunderstand and even fear mental disorders. Since educating yourself is one of the best ways to alleviate fear, let's look at the actual definition of a mental disorder.

According to the Surgeon General's Report, December 1999, a mental disorder is defined as "a health condition marked by alterations in thinking, mood, or behavior that causes distress or impairs a person's ability to function."

With this definition in mind, it's wise for you to take a comprehensive, objective look at your child's behavior. As scary as it might be to think about some of the things that could be going on, it's better to consider all the possibilities and to rule things out rather than to ignore possible explanations because you don't want them to be the answer. Information truly is power. Even if you're scared of what you're going to find, the more you know, the better you'll be able to help your child. If your child had any other type of brain disorder, there would be no question about doing everything you could to learn about it and treat the symptoms. So, let's approach a mental disorder the same way.

2

Could My Child Have a Mental Disorder?

♥

As hard as it is to consider the possibility of mental illness, there is no benefit to delaying diagnosis and treatment. If that's what it is, it's not going to go away on its own. Your child is not going to outgrow it. Early diagnosis and treatment are two of the greatest gifts you could ever give to your child. Most children make significant progress once their disorders are accurately identified and treatment has begun. Don't wait until you or your spouse feels emotionally ready to deal with it before you seek help. That day may never come. Also keep in mind that episodes of mental illness interrupt your child's normal psychological development and are extremely detrimental to self-esteem. Don't be afraid to take the next step. There is so much that can be done to make life better and easier for your child, your family, and for yourself!

In order to explore the possibility of a mental disorder you need to take a long, hard look at your child's behavior—not just the overall difficulty in your lives, but the individual, unique types of attitudes, actions and moods your child displays. The list of behaviors in this chapter can help you do this. Your job isn't to diagnose your child, either based on your own assessment or on the information in this or any other book. Instead, you need to gather information to take with you to a professional for evaluation and possible diagnosis and treatment of a mental disorder.

8

The following list will help you take a thorough and objective look at your child's behaviors. While many children exhibit some of the behaviors described in this chapter, children with Bipolar Disorder or some other mood or neuropsychological disorders exhibit many of them. They suffer to such an extreme that their ability to function is severely impaired. Their lives and the lives of their family members revolve around managing their moods and behaviors.

What Makes a Behavior a "Problem Behavior?"

▲ It interferes with doing other things.

▲ It interferes with positive interaction with peers and/or family members.

▲ It interferes with the family's ability to go out into the community.

▲ It inhibits learning and academic achievement.

▲ It limits participation in social activities.

▲ It inhibits success.

▲ It is dangerous to oneself or others.

▲ It makes family life unhappy.

▲ It is detrimental to the child's self esteem.

BEHAVIORS THAT MAY INDICATE BIPOLAR DISORDER AND/OR ANOTHER NEUROPSYCHOLOGICAL DISORDER

Even though all children may, at one time or another, display some of the following behaviors, keep in mind how the duration, frequency, intensity, and severity of your child's behavior differs from that of other children. Also keep in mind that this list contains possible symptoms. Your child may or may not experience each one. Just as no two "typical" children look alike, no two children with a behavioral disorder will be alike either, even if they end up with the same diagnosis.

As an infant, difficult to soothe and trouble sleeping

"The doctor told me Sara had colic, so I expected the screaming to stop by 3 months. She screamed almost all day long until she was 18 months old." (Bailey)

"Our son experienced extreme irritability from the day we brought him home. He cried for the first 12 weeks of life. He calmed down a little after that, but I still had to carry him in a Snuggli almost all the time, since he couldn't sleep at all unless I was holding him. Getting him to sleep at night became a several-hour-long ordeal. He couldn't calm down and hated being alone. Now that he's 7, he still hates being in his room and sleeping alone." (Lisa)

♥   Julie was extremely irritable from birth. She rarely slept and was inconsolable much of the time. Nothing I did seemed to make her feel better. I felt like such a failure. I watched all my friends with their babies and they seemed so happy compared to Julie. I lost confidence in being a new mom very quickly. Every experience, from changing a diaper, to feeding her, to visiting family seemed to be incredibly difficult.

Excessive sensitivity to sensory input

(Also see the *Sensory Integration Disorder* section in Chapter Four.)

"My 6 year-old daughter hears, smells, feels and tastes things so much more intensely than I do. She cannot tolerate tags in her clothing, fluorescent lighting or 'mushy' food. Sometimes seemingly minor things in the environment cause major amounts of distress or distraction." (Janet)

"Jeremy can't stand the grass. We spent months trying to get him used to it before he would walk on it without shoes on. Even at 7, he still tries to avoid playing on the lawn. He says he hates the feel of it." (Mike)

Severe separation anxiety that is more intense and lasts longer than the typical developmental phase

♥   As a toddler, Julie never left my side. She kept a superhuman grip on my leg. Even at 12 years old she is still attached to me like glue. She follows me wherever I go in the house or outside. When I have to go to the bathroom, *she lies outside the door and talks to me through the crack at the bottom. If I'm on the phone, I hide in the closet, backyard, garage, wherever. She broke the lock on my bedroom door so I can't take a "time-out." She never plays alone or entertains herself. The thought of being alone fills Julie with dread and anxiety.*

"Getting 8 year-old Ryan to sleep at night can be a two hour ordeal. He hates being alone in his room and I often wake up to find him asleep on the floor at the foot of my bed. Even during the day he won't let me out of his sight. When he is playing with friends, I have to be in the same room or he will just leave the friends and follow me. When he was a baby he would take all his naps on my lap. Being alone in his crib made him cry so hard. It was almost as if he was in a panic, and I was so desperate for him to sleep that I would have done anything." (Annie)

Precocious

"David met all his developmental milestones early. He skipped crawling and walked at 8 months. He was talking like a little grown-up by age two. He started to read when he was three." (Payton)

"Tim could get into anything, anywhere. I couldn't leave any door unlocked. Baby gates and playpens were useless after he was 8 months old. He could climb over them. By the time he was 9 months old, he could open all the 'baby-proof' cabinet locks. When he was one, he would open the cabinets and drawers and use them to climb up on top of the counters." (Andie)

♥ *Even when her peers were barely putting together sentences, Julie was asking complex questions like, "Where did the first person come from?" She wanted to understand things, complicated things. She didn't accept simple answers.*

Easily frustrated

"Not being able to reach a toy, push a button, or put a shoe on can send Daria, 5, into a rage. It's almost like she is angry with her body for not being able to do what she wants it to do." (David)

♥   *Asking Julie to do a simple task is taking a big risk. If she's doing something else or isn't in the mood, a total meltdown is a good possibility. She will start crying before she even attempts the task. It's the same with homework. She just looks at the page and starts to cry and say self-deprecating things or gets so angry that she starts yelling at me. Even if she tries a problem, she gets so frustrated there's no possibility of ever getting it done.*

Behavior is at its worst at home

"Matthew's 5th grade teacher describes him as a sweet, quiet boy. Little does she know that five minutes after getting home from school he is screaming, hitting the walls, and calling me names. I'll never understand how he can be so good at school and fall apart the moment he sees me. I'd love to see Matt through her eyes. I'd also love for her to experience what I deal with." (Diane)

"I think the reason Derek, who is 7, falls apart the second he gets home is that he's tried so hard to hold it together all day in school that he just can't hold on any more. He knows he is safe and loved at home, that's where he can let go. While I wish he could sometimes control himself with me, I'm glad that he knows I'll love him no matter what." (Maria)

♥   *When Julie was in first grade, her teacher thought I was out of my mind for having her on medication. She saw Julie as a cute, shy, attentive student. I actually had a friend, whose son was in the same class, talk to her and confirm that what I was saying about Julie's behavior at home was true.*

Pressured speech and racing thoughts

"In one breath, 5 year-old Lissa can say, 'I want a bike for Christmas. Do you like broccoli? What makes boats float?' Sometimes her thoughts are coming so fast, she can't even finish one sentence before she starts another one." (Pamela)

"One night after 8 year-old John came out of his room for what felt like the millionth time, I yelled, 'Why can't you just go to sleep?' He calmly looked at me and said, 'because I'm thinking about trains, what I like to eat, how I'm afraid of someone crawling in my window, my friend Ryan, how to rearrange

my room, and what I want to play with, all at the same time. That makes it hard to fall asleep.'" (Samantha)

"Rebecca's thoughts seem to get in the way of her getting things done. When she was 9 she told me that she wished she had a button that would turn off part of her brain. Another time she told her teacher she couldn't do her work because her head wouldn't shut up." (Rachel)

Frequent, rapid and dramatic changes in mood

"My 11 year-old daughter can be laughing and happily involved in an activity, then all of a sudden, seemingly for no reason at all, she becomes extremely sad and talks about wanting to die." (Rhiannon)

"After an hour of raging that included a broken patio door and a broken window, 8 year-old Adam's mood changed as if a switch was flipped. Suddenly he was hugging me, kissing me, and telling me how much he loves me." (Steve)

Moods that are intense and extreme

♥   *There never seems to be any middle ground with Julie. She is either the queen of the world or she is the lowest life form on the planet. She can either be so silly and happy that she's out of control, or she is so sad or angry that she's a danger to herself or others.*

Inappropriate energy and activity level

"There are times when Brianna, 10, is certifiably hyper. She exhausts you just by watching her. She seems to be 'bouncing off the walls.' She's loud, inappropriate and talks a mile a minute." (Crystal)

"My daughter has always been extremely active. I hate it when other parents say that their children are really active, too. Those people have no idea what active looks like. Their kids look like they are in slow motion compared to my daughter." (Denise)

"Brandon has never been able to stay still. The closest he can get is watching TV while sitting on his bouncy horse. That way, he's moving, but he's in one place." (Monica)

"9 year-old Tiana's energy levels often seem like they're the total opposite of everyone else's. She's wide awake and bouncing around at 11 p.m. and is tired and cranky at 8 in the morning." (Marianne)

Manipulative, controlling behavior

"If I were married to someone who treats me as badly as Sara does, I would have been divorced years ago. Her controlling, manipulative, harassing, bitchy behavior is unbearable to be around. She's bossy, mischievous, loud, and obnoxious, never plays with anything, has no sense of personal space, and is too rough and aggressive. She's only 6." (Toni)

♥   *People are Julie's toys. She's like the puppet master and we are the puppets. She tries to control everything. You can see her trying to manipulate other people's behaviors, and it seems to be not only to get what she wants, but also for the sheer pleasure of it. She does it with friends, her family, her teachers, and even her therapist and psychiatrist.*

Frequent irritability

"Any little thing triggers 9 year-old Tara's temper. Even if her brother is just minding his own business, she acts like he's intentionally trying to irritate her. Of course, she never thinks that her behavior could possibly be bothering someone else! We often feel like we're walking on eggshells to avoid catching her attention." (Clarice)

"Jared is the grumpiest child I have ever met. His mood can be so foul and unpleasant. It's a strange thing to see such a young person act like a grumpy old man!" (Donna)

Extremely provocative, ability to elicit strong emotional responses in others

♥   *Whether the interactions with Julie are positive or negative ones, the power and intensity of them never ceases to amaze me. It takes everything I have sometimes to keep myself from hopping on the top or the bottom of the roller coaster with her.*

"It doesn't matter whether someone is happy with him or furious with him, my son will do whatever it takes to get a response." (Kelly)

Unresponsive to discipline

♥ *I've tried every type of discipline known to man with Julie. How is it possible that nothing works? Not only does her behavior not improve, it actually gets worse.*

"7 year-old David repeatedly yells mean and nasty words. I've tried everything from spanking to time out to taking things away from him. He just doesn't care. He doesn't care about any consequence I threaten. When I follow through, he just keeps on doing whatever he wants." (Marsha)

Inability to tolerate submission

♥ *Julie would rather fight to the death than give in to me. She HATES being told what to do. She'll choose an hour or more in her room over following a direction. It's as if she sees it as humiliation to do as I say. And don't even think about winning a game if you're playing with her, the board will be sent flying across the room.*

"8 year-old Cole's worst behavior seems to start when I tell him to do something. He just can't stand being told what to do. He can't even handle casual suggestions about what to do. He'll do the exact opposite just to spite me." (Janie)

Difficulty controlling anger

♥ *Julie doesn't get mad . . . she rages.*

"Jeremy, 4, goes from zero to sixty in a matter of seconds. There's usually no stopping him and his anger seems so disproportionate to the situation." (Elyssa)

"There is no difference in 10 year-old Erin's level of anger over a little thing and a major crisis. It's either all or nothing. And her 'all' is extremely intense. I can't even imagine being that angry, that often." (Dana)

Threatening, aggressive and/or violent episodes

"Sometimes I'm afraid to go to sleep because my 5 year-old son's behavior is so out of control, I'm scared he'll get up in the middle of the night and hurt *himself or his brother. To be perfectly honest, I'm afraid he might hurt me, too."* (Robin)

"John, 6, has been very aggressive lately. He's been hitting me and calling me horrible names. Yesterday, he came up behind me and hit me hard with a book. I actually have a black and blue mark. If I did to my child what he's done to me, I'd be in jail for child abuse." (Donna)

"Jamie, 11, is very violent towards her things. She'll throw things at the wall, break things on purpose, and destroy anything in her path." (Kevin)

"Caleb's violence starting with throwing things and advanced to hitting me, his little sister and his father. It got really scary when he was 8 and pushed his sister down the stairs. He's kicked the dog several times for doing something like breathing on his pizza. He's also choked his sister hard enough to leave marks on several occasions." (Madison)

♥ *One day when Julie was 6 years old she was angry with me for putting her in time out. It was very quiet upstairs for quite a while, which was very unusual, so I went upstairs to check on her. I found that she had placed about fifty hairpins at the top of the stairs, positioning each one so that it stuck straight up out of the carpet. It was basically a booby trap meant for me to step on. I was shocked not only at the maliciousness, but also at the amount of time and patience (not her forte) it must have taken to accomplish it.*

Prolonged and intense temper tantrums

♥ *We had almost three years of terrible tantrums. At least once a day Julie would tantrum for up to two hours. She would scream and writhe around on the ground. She has this super-human strength and would often strike out at me or destroy her room. I actually called our psychologist once and just held out the phone so she could hear for herself what we were dealing with. There were many occasions when I had to restrain Julie to keep her from hurting me. She would kick me, hit, pinch, bite, spit, even head butt. Occasionally, she would actually foam at the mouth. I didn't even know that was a real thing until I saw my daughter do it, and it was horrifying. She gets this feral look in her eyes that is almost primal. It's like she's going to explode, like she's fighting for her life.*

"When Jeremy is raging, he screams non-stop for hours, destroys his room, repeatedly bangs doors, kicks the walls and is absolutely tireless. Our home bears the scars of his rages like holes in the walls, broken door hinges and cracked mirrors. I'd be thrilled if my child had the kind of temper tantrums that other kids have. I could cope with him throwing himself on the floor and crying—even if he is 6 instead of 2!" (Jamie)

"Dillon doesn't have temper tantrums. He has rages. A tantrum is something a 2-year old or a spoiled child does when he doesn't get his way. Dillon screams, throws furniture, destroys anything he touches, kicks, punches, bites, and hits. We still keep our house baby-proofed even though he's 9 years old. At least it slows him down a little. I'm terrified he's going to hurt himself or someone else while he's destroying the house. The intensity and power are unbelievable." (Shannon)

Poor impulse control

♥   *Julie doesn't seem to have the ability to think before she speaks or acts. Whatever comes into her mind she says it, without any regard for others' feelings. She tells people they are fat, have bad breath, or are bald or wrinkled. This has caused many uncomfortable, embarrassing moments. It's not always like she wants to hurt people, she just doesn't seem to have that little voice in her brain that says, "You shouldn't say that," like other people do.*

"If Becky sees something she wants to touch she can't seem to stop herself. She cannot take turns and standing in a line is a nightmare. I had expected this type of behavior when she was 3, but not when she's 8." (Morgan)

Unusually high energy, restlessness and problems with concentration and attention span

♥   *There are definitely times when I want to glue Julie to a chair. She can't seem to sit still or concentrate long enough to accomplish even the simplest of tasks. She changes activities frequently and almost always needs help finding things to do. Sometimes she literally runs laps around the house. She's tireless.*

"Madelyn, 9, can't participate in group activities or sports. She can't stay still while instructions are given or while she's waiting her turn to do

something. She just runs around or tries to do things when it's not her turn. It's just not worth the anxiety to keep trying. It doesn't end up being fun for her, so we just don't bother anymore." (Erica)

Uninhibited behavior, doesn't follow unwritten rules of appropriate social conduct

"My 9 year-old son behaves like there are absolutely no boundaries. He's climbed on top of tables at restaurants, pulled out (and sat on) a whoopee cushion at a parent/teacher conference, and goes behind the counters at stores to take things he wants right out of the cases." (Carla)

Explosive and unpredictable temper, suddenly getting upset or acting out for no apparent reason

"My 8 year-old daughter's attitude is 'hit first, ask questions later.' She'll be playing sweetly with her brother, then, if the game doesn't go her way or he makes a noise that bothers her, he's suddenly crying and she's furious. There's no period of escalation when they're starting to bother each other. Jason doesn't like to play with her anymore because he never knows when he's suddenly going to get punched. There's no warning." (Nancy)

♥ *I always have an anxious feeling when I'm with Julie, even when things are going well. I think it's because I never know when I'm going to say or do something that will set her off. It's like walking through a minefield.*

Verbally abusive

"My 12 year-old says things to me that I wouldn't say to my worst enemy. I am his verbal punching bag. Mean, nasty, hateful words just pour from his mouth. He feels great when he's done and wants to hug and kiss me and tell me that he loves me. I feel like I've been hit by a truck." (Paula)

"This kid that I do so much for frequently tells me that I never do anything for him, that he hates me and that I'm the worst mother in the world. He's even called me a 'stupid bitch.' He's only 6. I hate to think of what he's going to say when he's older." (Marissa)

Highly oppositional and antagonistic

"My daughter has just gotten up and walked out of the room while the principal was talking to her. She's also ripped up assignments right in front of her 3rd grade teacher." (Katie)

♥ Everything with Julie seems to be a battle. She argues for the sake of arguing and seems to long for that type of interaction, especially with her father and me. She can be extremely mean-spirited and seems to enjoy "getting a rise" out of other people. She is incredibly argumentative. She will argue that the sky is green until she's blue in the face. She looks for things to fight about, and she will provoke an argument or confrontation with any willing participant.

Grandiosity—unrealistic beliefs in one's abilities and powers

♥ Julie sees no difference between herself and adults other than that she's shorter. She has no inherent respect for adults or authority figures. It makes no sense to her why she should have to listen or follow an adult's direction. It was clear she even felt this way when she was a toddler.

"When 7 year-old Rachel is manic she truly believes she can fly. I have to physically keep her from jumping out the window. She is not trying to hurt herself at these times. She really thinks she can fly around the neighborhood." (Sandra)

"David, 10, thinks he's 'above the law.' Things may be illegal or against the rules for others, but not for him. One day, an officer came to the house to talk to him about stealing a bike. He wasn't even intimidated by the police!" (Karen)

Poor judgment or risky behavior

"Brandon, 9, gets sheer pleasure from activities that are unsafe. He climbs on the roof, goes up the staircase on the outside of the banister, and hangs out of windows. He's having a ball while I'm scared to death." (Allison)

"Jessie decided one day that she wanted to be at home instead of in school. The teacher thought she left to go to the bathroom. She left the school, crossed *several major streets, and walked four miles to get home. She's 7 years old."* (Lonnie)

"I was working in the yard one day when Jeremy was 6 years old. I heard a noise, looked up and saw Jeremy walking across the roof of the house. Afterwards, I asked him why he did that. He said he was upstairs and was hot so he wanted to get some air." (Diana)

Self-deprecating

"What am I supposed to say when my 7 year-old son says, 'You hate me. You wish I was dead. I hate myself. I am the stupidest person on the planet'?" (Jordan)

♥ *Sometimes I actually say to Julie, "Don't you talk about my daughter like that!" She will talk about how ugly, stupid, "idiotic," or worthless she is. It is so heartbreaking to look at her and see that she really believes what she is saying. No matter what I say, I cannot seem to make her feel better and usually just have to wait for it to pass.*

Sad, empty moods

"Cameron, 8, feels so sad at times, as if nothing is going right and no one loves or cares about him. He wanders around the house not really knowing what to do with himself. He's very pessimistic at these times and moves at a very slow pace." (Nelly)

Thoughts of suicide and/or death

"Justin first talked about killing himself when he was 4 years old. I cannot even begin to describe the horror I feel every time I think not only about my child taking his life, but also my child feeling terrible enough inside to even think or wish it." (Judy)

"When the other 6 year-olds were curious about and scared of death, Adam was thinking of and planning ways to 'make himself dead.'" (Claudia)

♥ *Julie was 5 when she started talking about taking her own life. It started out as, "I wish I was dead" or, "Everyone would be so much happier if I were dead." She then began to talk about how she would do it. She talked a lot about jumping out the window and even opened it a few times. Other times she talked about getting a knife out of the kitchen and cutting her head off or jumping out of the car while it was going really fast. This scares me to death. What if she does it? What if she does something else? . . . I could think of a thousand "what if's." They all scare me to death.*

Egocentric—everything happens to and for them

♥ *No matter what happens or whom it involves, Julie perceives the situation as being about her. If I pay attention to her cousin who fell off a bike, she tells me that I must not love her because I'm paying attention to someone else. If the store is out of her favorite type of muffin, she's convinced that they did it on purpose to bother her. If I'm out one evening with a friend, she's sure it's because I wanted to get away from her.*

Difficulty with empathy, sympathy, remorse and emotions that relate to others' feelings

"In Lauren's case, apologizing is torture. Looking at things from other people's perspectives is virtually impossible, even though she should be able to now that she's 10. No matter how hard I try to explain how her actions affect others, she can only understand how they make her feel." (Nina)

"John, 8, thinks it's funny when someone else's feelings get hurt, but when someone does something that makes him feel bad, he thinks they should be put in jail. Even if the other child did exactly the same thing that John did, he just doesn't see the similarities. He only cares about what happens to him." (Jenna)

Intentionally hurtful toward others

♥ *Julie physically and emotionally hurts me on a regular basis. She'll jump on my back without warning, smack me hard on the butt, or grab me around the neck. She tells me that I'm fat and that my clothes are ugly. It seems like she's purposely trying to hurt me. When I explain how I feel about what she's doing or tell her that she's hurt me, she ignores me. Sometimes she immediately repeats the behavior.*

"My daughter's best friend met her at the door of the preschool with a huge grin on his face. He held out his hand and offered her some treats and told her that he had saved them especially for her. She grabbed them, dropped them on the floor, and smashed them with her foot. You should have seen the hurt look on his face. She thought it was funny. I was mortified." (Amelia)

Crying for little or no reason

♥   *Julie spends much of her free time crying. I feel incredibly sad for her. Most of the things she cries about are so insignificant that I don't know how to reply to her logically. A stuck zipper, a simple "no," a crooked bedspread, or telling her it's time to eat can make her start to cry. As a matter of fact, she usually wakes up crying in the morning.*

Sleep problems, including night terrors and dramatic fluctuations in the desired and required amount of sleep

"I feel like a new mother. How much sleep I get depends on how much my 7 year-old sleeps. Some nights he'll sleep two hours then wake up smiling and ready for a new day. Other times, he wants to sleep practically all day and is up all night. Unfortunately, there's no way to predict how much sleep he'll need on any given day." (Jennifer)

"When Becky, 6, has a nightmare, it's so intense that she keeps experiencing the dream even after she's awake. She says she can see the blood and feel the pain." (Rebecca)

"Nine year-old Abby spends many nights remodeling her room. It's bedtime, but she will spend hours moving her furniture, reorganizing her bookshelf, or lining up her beanie babies. She is not mad or upset, she just seems to have this energy inside that she has to 'do something.' To lie in bed seems virtually impossible." (Maureen)

"I keep the baby monitor in my 10 year-old son's room—hidden, of course, so he won't turn it off. If I hear the sound of his breathing, I know that he's sleeping. If I hear him get up, I immediately go check on him. I never know what he'll do, even in the middle of the night." (Quincee)

Lying

♥   *Julie is a gifted liar. She'll look me straight in the face and swear that she didn't eat the purple Popsicle when her lips are bright purple. When I point this out to her and show her the empty wrapper in the trash, she still denies it. Sometimes I think she lies just for the fun of it. It's another one of the ways she uses people as toys. Lying seems to be one of her favorite pastimes.*

Intrusive behavior

"My 8 year-old son has what we call, 'in your face' behavior. He'll literally get an inch from your face when he talks to you or he'll stick what he's trying to show you right in your face. He doesn't seem to understand the concept of personal space and almost enjoys making us uncomfortable in that way." (Larry)

Problems with peers

♥   *Making and keeping friends has been a constant struggle for Julie. People initially seem drawn to her, but quickly lose interest. She's bossy, unable to compromise, inflexible, and is only interested in what she wants to do. She thinks nothing of saying, "I don't want to play with you anymore. Go home," or calling her friend a "stupid jerk." The next day she'll expect that friend to want to play with her again.*

Loss of touch with reality or hallucinations

"At times my daughter can't tell the difference between what's going on in her head and what's real. One time, she kept talking about how she had to feed the dog before she went to school. She even poured cereal into a bowl and put it on the floor to feed the dog. She was looking and looking for a dog, but we don't have one and it was summer break. It scared me to death." (Jackie)

"Today we were having a wonderful time playing together when suddenly my 5 year-old daughter said, 'Mom, that other little girl is crying.' I asked, 'What other little girl?' She said, 'That other little girl who lives in our house. I can hear her crying.' There isn't any other girl who lives in our house." (Alicia)

"Before Michelle went on medication, when she was 8, she would see bugs crawling up the wall when nothing was there. Another time she saw a man in her room. It was terrifying for both of us." (Lynne)

Hypersexuality and provocative behavior

"Abby tries to act 'sexy' with very provocative body movements. She sometimes tries to kiss her dad or me in a very inappropriate manner. She also tries to touch my breasts. It doesn't seem right for such a young child (it started when she was 6) to act in such a blatantly sexual way." (Stacey)

"It's embarrassing to admit this, but my 7 year-old masturbates a lot. He sometimes tries to do it in front of us, and I have to make him go to his room. What if he ever tries to do it at school or someone else's home?" (Elena)

"My 9 year-old son has times when he's obsessed with sexual words and behavior. Last night he wrote me a note that said, 'Want to do it all night long, baby?'" (Anna)

Inappropriate urination

"I have caught Joanne, 6, peeing in the dirty laundry basket and have found spots in the corner of her room between the dresser and the wall where she has peed. She has a bathroom right next to her room. It's so disturbing." (Kimberly)

"One day, when Kelly was 8, she was so angry with me she stood in front of me, looked me square in the eye and peed all over herself." (Stephanie)

Craving for carbohydrates and sweets

"If Melissa, 8, had her way, she would eat candy and noodles and nothing else." (Sallie)

♥   *Sometimes I find Julie in the pantry with the door closed. She'll be in there eating sugar or spoonfuls of frosting. I have found wrappers from baking chocolate and huge amounts of hoarded candy and cereal in her room. It's odd because I am not usually restrictive about what she eats (although I doubt I would OK sugar out of the bowl). I'm not sure why she feels like she has to hide.*

Regular difficulty in the mornings

"The part of the day I dread the most is in the morning when I have to wake up 7 year-old Jake to get ready for school. The house becomes totally stressful instantaneously. He has a terrible time getting out of bed. He says he's too tired to get up and literally starts crying before his eyes even open. A typical morning can consist of an hour or more of crying and falling apart over basic things like dressing, eating, brushing teeth, etc. I usually feel like going back to bed by the time he leaves for school." (Candace)

"Waking up Kevin, 12, has always been like waking up a hibernating grizzly. It's literally like trying to wake someone up who's in the middle of his deepest sleep. It takes a long time to wake him, and then he's incredibly groggy for an hour. It's almost like he has a hangover. I've dressed him many times while he's lying in bed. Sometimes I have to physically pull him out of bed to get him on his feet. He finally seems to be starting to wake up when we walk out the door for school." (Cheryl)

"I'm actually jealous when my friends complain about how early their 5 year-olds wake them up. Jenna is up so much during the night that it's next to impossible to get her to wake up the next morning. It's a battle every single day. It's okay for us to be a little bit late for pre-school, but I worry about what will happen when she's in real school next year." (Trisha)

Cruelty to animals

"My son used to do awful things to my cat. When he was 8, he taped its legs together with masking tape and tried to shut the door on its tail. He would kick it and annoy it when we weren't looking." (Tammi)

"My 11 year-old loves terrorizing the dog. His latest torture was throwing her into the freezing cold swimming pool." (Jeff)

Self-injurious behavior

"When she was 10, my daughter went through a period of a few months when she pulled out her hair. We began to notice patches of her scalp showing. Then she started on her eyebrows and even her eyelashes. It was so awful. It literally made me sick to my stomach. You cannot imagine the horror of watching your child harm herself unless you've been there." (Amy)

♥ *It started with a loud, repetitive thud. When I went upstairs to see what it was, I discovered 10 year-old Julie banging her head against the wall over and over again. Her head was bleeding and there was a hole in the wall. When I asked her why she did it, she said, "I don't know. I don't know." No matter how much we talk about other ways to handle her frustrations, she can't seem to stop doing it. Just when I thought I had her repertoire all figured out, she added something new and I realized that I might never be able to predict what she'll do next.*

If your experience of parenting has been like what we described in the first chapter and your child's behavior fits many of the descriptions in this chapter, it is worth taking the next step and having your child professionally evaluated. You may have been through this evaluation process before. You may already have discussed your child's behavior with a doctor or doctors. You may have been dismissed with a pat on the back and a "she just needs more structure," a "boys will be boys," or a "she'll grow out of it" type response. You must still have doubts, though, or you wouldn't be reading this book. If you were concerned that your child had a serious physical illness, you would get a second opinion, and a third opinion, and as many opinions as you needed until you felt comfortable that you had the correct information. Let's take the same approach. You must keep trying until you get what you need to help your child. Getting a diagnosis is a big part of getting these needs met.

3
Getting a Diagnosis

WHAT A DIAGNOSIS IS

Diagnosis can be a scary thing. It means that a professional has acknowledged that there is something going on with your child beyond just being different or difficult—something that must be treated. While this can seem like a negative at first, we encourage you to get as accurate a diagnosis as possible, even if you're uncomfortable with the concept of "labeling" a child and fear that others will treat your child differently once she's been diagnosed. You probably have a part of you that is afraid, as well as a part of you that is desperate to figure out what's really going on. Getting a diagnosis is a critical step in improving your child's life.

What is a Diagnosis?

▲ A diagnosis is a shorthand way to describe a group of symptoms.

▲ A diagnosis is a way of communicating these symptoms between professionals.

▲ A diagnosis is a working hypothesis of your child's behaviors.

▲ Most importantly, a diagnosis enables your child to qualify for certain types of healthcare, insurance, public assistance, and school accommodations.

FINDING THE DOCTOR TO DIAGNOSE YOUR CHILD

To get the diagnosis, you need to get some professional help. There are a variety of types of professionals who are trained to do mental evaluations. A psychiatrist is a physician who deals with the diagnosis, treatment, and prevention of mental and emotional disorders, including prescribing and managing psychiatric medications. A psychologist is a professional, but not a physician, who specializes in mental processes and behaviors including diagnosis, testing, and treatment for mental, behavioral, and/or emotional disorders. Therapists, counselors and social workers are professionals who provide a variety of assessment and therapy services.

When your child exhibits multiple problem behaviors and Bipolar Disorder is a possible diagnosis, your best bet is to go to a psychiatrist, preferably one who specializes in children. These professionals have the most comprehensive training and the ability to prescribe medication. To find a psychiatrist who will diagnosis your child, ask for referrals from professionals who seem sympathetic to what you're going through. This might include your pediatrician and the school psychologist or counselor. You can also contact local psychiatric hospitals, your insurance company's list of providers, a mental health support group, National Alliance for the Mentally Ill (see NAMI in the *Additional Resources* section), the local psychiatric society (look in the yellow pages under Associations), or online physician directories. Even better, if you know anyone who has a child with difficulties, he/she may be able to offer suggestions about where to start.

Of course, if you're in an HMO or other managed care, you might not be able to go straight to a psychiatrist. You might have to get a referral from your child's primary care physician before you can see a mental health professional. There also might be limits on the type or amount of mental healthcare your child can use. You'll have to keep working the system in order to get to a doctor who can make a diagnosis. If your child is diagnosed with certain mental disorders, however, the rules change. Bipolar Disorder and some other mental illnesses are legally considered biologically-based. This means they are physical illnesses, not emotional states. So, by law, your insurance has to cover them like any other physical disorder. Mental health coverage limitations should not apply. (Please see Chapter Eleven for suggestions on dealing with insurance.) This is a good example of how important it is to have a formal diagnosis. It can dramatically affect your insurance benefits.

Most people diagnosed with a mental illness experienced symptoms for years before they were properly diagnosed. Our children don't have that kind of time to waste, so don't just assume any psychiatrist is the right one. As you may already have found out from previous experiences with doctors and just as you would with any other type of health issues, you need to screen doctors to find the best one for you and your child.

> *"I can't believe I have to go through this again. Zack has already been assessed by a pediatrician, the school psychologist and a psychiatrist. The treatment for their diagnosis of ADHD just isn't working. His lack of attention at school isn't the only problem that needs to be addressed, but it's all they think about. I just know something else is going on, but they seem to think Ritalin is the answer. I'm going to have to start all over with a new psychiatrist and try to get to the bottom of this." (Joan)*

Some doctors (we're using this term to mean any healthcare professional who can make a diagnosis) offer a free initial consultation. When scheduling a time to meet, ask to set a free consultation, rather than an appointment. If a doctor won't provide a free initial meeting, ask if you can talk awhile on the phone before you schedule an actual appointment. Plan on consulting with or talking to as many doctors as it takes to find one that feels right. You won't want to bring your child to any initial meetings. You will want to be able to talk freely. You don't want your child go through needless appointments with doctors that you decide aren't the right fit. The goal is for you to evaluate the doctor to determine whether he or she is the right one to work with your child. Even though the doctor should be asking some questions about your child, this is really your conversation. You should be prepared to ask questions as well.

Questions To Ask Doctors:

▲ What is your expertise in childhood emotional and behavioral issues?

▲ What is your experience with childhood-onset Bipolar Disorder and other neurodevelopment disorders?

If you are happy with the doctor's answers to the previous two questions, continue on with the rest. If not, go on to the next doctor.

▲ How do you stay current on the latest research on mental illness in children?

▲ What are the steps in the diagnostic process?

▲ What information will you need from me? What information will you need from my child's other parent?

▲ How do I schedule appointments? How quickly can I usually get my child in for an appointment when she needs one that isn't already scheduled?

▲ How do you handle insurance?

▲ Would you be available by phone or pager when I need you?

▲ What is your on-call coverage? Do you share call with another doctor?

▲ What is your approach to prescribing medication? When do you think it's appropriate to give psychiatric medication to a child? When isn't it?

▲ Are you willing to be involved in communicating with my child's school and teachers?

▲ How familiar are you with other forms of treatment, such as day treatment or special school programs?

Qualities to Look for in a Doctor:

When you first talk with the doctor, be aware of how well the doctor does the following:

▲ Seems supportive and attentive

▲ Encourages you to ask questions and provide information

▲ Asks you for information about your child

▲ Seems knowledgeable about childhood neurodevelopmental disorders

▲ Seems to welcome and encourage your involvement in your child's treatment

▲ Listens with interest and respect

▲ Develops a good rapport with you and seems interested in meeting your child

▲ Communicates in a manner that you understand and that makes you feel comfortable

▲ Leaves you feeling like you're on the right path

▲ Doesn't rush you, makes you feel like he/she has the time to help

---

PREPARING FOR YOUR FIRST APPOINTMENT

Once you've selected the doctor, it's time to prepare for your first appointment. If you haven't already found out, ask the doctor what will happen at this meeting so you can prepare yourself as well as your child. Ask whether you should go alone or with your child. What information does the doctor want from you and how does he/she want you to provide it? What will the doctor do with your child when they're together? Will you be in the room with your child the whole time or part of the time?

"I told 8 year-old Joe that he was going to visit a doctor who specializes in brain chemicals and how they control behavior. We talked about how he had

seen a pediatrician who takes care of his body, a dentist who takes care of his teeth, and an ophthalmologist who takes care of his eyes. He was totally comfortable with the idea of going to a psychiatrist who will take care of his brain. I also explained that since the doctor can't see or touch his brain, the only way to figure out what is going on in his brain it to talk about his behavior and feelings." (Sammy)

The next step is to prepare to give a full, honest and accurate description of your child's behavior. Because visiting a doctor, and especially a psychiatric doctor, can be a nerve-wracking experience, it's a good idea to rely on more than just your memory. If you haven't already, make a list of behaviors that you think are a problem. List your specific concerns. Jot down notes about specific examples of when your child was at her worst. You can even use the list in Chapter Two as a checklist and bring it in with you. Make sure you don't minimize or exaggerate, just be as descriptive as you can. The doctor relies heavily on your description of your child's behaviors, so being prepared makes this much easier. You may be in the habit of trying to minimize the severity of your child's problems when you talk to other people, but this isn't time or place to make a five-car pileup sound like a fender-bender.

"We finally got a diagnosis after years of trying to figure out what was going on with Michelle. We were convinced that 'something wasn't normal,' but couldn't get anyone to take us seriously. When someone did pay some attention, we'd solve a small piece of the puzzle, but never felt like we had the big picture figured out. The way we finally got a diagnosis was keeping a written record of her moods and behaviors. We documented every aspect of how she was at specific times of the day, how she slept, how she behaved in difficult situations and when she seemed particularly upset or unusually active. Then we found a doctor who was able to look at the information and clearly see what the problem was. By writing everything down we were able to communicate with the doctor and provide all the information he needed for an accurate diagnosis." (Karly)

Other Ways to Prepare for Your First Appointment:

In addition to finding out how the doctor handles the first visit, telling your child what to expect, and preparing notes on your child's behavior, here are some other steps you should take:

▲ If necessary, make sure you have a referral from your child's primary care physician.

▲ Make sure the doctor has your child's complete medical record. This may require submitting a written request to your pediatrician to transfer a copy of the records. Follow up at least a few days before the appointment to make sure it was received.

▲ Be prepared to answer questions about your pregnancy, labor and delivery as well as any illnesses your child may have had and when he met many of his developmental milestones. If you filled out a baby book with information on when your child first walked, said a word, and made other developmental achievements, you could even bring that. If not, look back through your photo albums, talk with a grandparent, or try to remember the approximate dates of major medical and developmental milestones.

▲ Since many disorders are genetic, do some thinking about your family history. Do you have any relatives with mental health problems, suicide, substance abuse, depression, or alcohol related problems? You might even want to think about family members' medication histories, driving records, money handling skills, marital histories and eccentric behaviors. It may even be worth a call to a family member who might be able to recall some information you may not think of or know. These family histories can help identify possible undiagnosed cases of Bipolar Disorder or other mental illnesses in your family tree. It's extremely important to get as many details as possible because previous generations didn't have the benefit of current, well-defined diagnoses. Disorders may be remembered by family members as "nervous breakdowns," or a relative who always was moody or had "the blues," or earlier terminology like "manic depressive." If you can find out what medication someone was given, your doctor might have a better idea about what types of symptoms your relative exhibited and be able to spot similarities in your child.

▲ Be prepared to talk about your own mental health history and prepare your spouse for the same.

▲ Think about the possibility of medications. It's important that you keep an open mind. If you can prepare yourself enough emotionally to discuss it, you will be able to ask questions and get a feel for the doctor's philosophies about medication. You'll want to be close to being on the same page about how aggressive or conservative you want to be. Share your feelings and concerns with the doctor. We will talk about what you need to know about medications in Chapter Eight.

▲ Both parents should be at the meeting since you may have different perspectives and memories about your child's behavior. It's also helpful for both parents to hear first-hand what the doctor has to say.

▲ Bring a pad to take notes or, if the doctor is comfortable with the idea, tape-record your meeting so you can refer back to the information later.

▲ Reassure yourself that taking your child to a doctor for a mental health evaluation isn't committing yourself to any particular course of action. If there isn't a diagnosable mental illness, at least you'll know, so you can start exploring other ways to help your child. If there is, you'll be able to start making effective treatment decisions.

"My girlfriend gave me a lot of reassurance about taking Melanie to a psychiatrist. She reminded me of when Melanie had hurt her finger in PE and I debated whether I should take her to the doctor for an x-ray. I finally decided that if it was broken and I had done nothing, I would be far worse off than if I took her in and nothing was wrong. Either way, going to the doctor wasn't going to change whether or not it was broken. I had to look at going to a psychiatrist the same way I would going to any other medical doctor." (Linda)

"My 7 year-old son Joey, came into my room at 10:00 one night and told me that he hated the thoughts in his head. When I encouraged him to talk, he told me that sometimes he gets so mad that he has to bite himself. He said that he knows that there's no reason to be mad, but he can't help feeling that way. He really wanted help. On top of this comment, which broke my heart, he had been obsessively and uncontrollably doing a complex finger-licking routine multiple times every day for about a month. I knew I needed to have him assessed, especially since there's a family history of Obsessive

Compulsive Disorder, but 'get psychiatrist appointment for Joey' sat on my to-do list for a few days. In fact, after a week, Joey even asked me if I had talked to the doctor yet. I felt horrible because even though I thought I was totally comfortable with the thought of a child going to a psychiatrist, I had a very hard time getting myself to do it. Once I talked to the pediatrician, got some referrals, figured out my insurance situation, and actually started making calls, I felt a wonderful sense of control replace the anxious feelings I had been having. When I found a psychiatrist and told him that I needed to find out whether or not Joey has a 'something' that needs to be dealt with, he told me that my description of Joey's symptoms were some classic signs of OCD. I made my list of concerns and actually looked forward to the first appointment. Joey gave me a huge hug when I told him that I had made an appointment for him to talk to a doctor who could help him with the bad thoughts in his head." (Sheryl)

"I had such mixed feelings about taking Talia to a psychiatrist. I was embarrassed, relieved and terrified all at once. I was even nervous that I was going to be told that I just wasn't being a good parent. I knew in my heart that her behavior was uncontrollable and the pediatrician agreed that going to a psychiatrist was a good next step, but I kept worrying about what I would do next if this doctor told me there was nothing he could do for us. I can't even describe how it felt to have the psychiatrist pat my shoulder and tell me that I had done the right thing by bringing Talia in and that he thought he could help us." (Keisha)

♥ I began to seek out professional help when Julie was 5. She needed formal IQ testing to remain in the gifted program she had been in since she was 3 1/2. I was referred to a wonderful psychologist. Before I knew it, I was spilling my guts to her about my troubles with Julie. She seemed to understand so much about Julie with very little explanation. I felt as if someone was grabbing a side of a huge box I had been carrying alone up to this point. Suddenly my load felt a little lighter. This was the beginning of my journey into the unknown world of Bipolar Disorder.

DIAGNOSING BIPOLAR DISORDER

Diagnosing mental disorders can be very difficult. This is especially true for Bipolar Disorder. There is no blood test, X-ray, or physical exam that can be used to determine if the illness is present. Its symptoms aren't easy to understand and can't be seen with the naked eye. Diagnosis is often more a process of elimination and trial and error than anything else. It is all based on behavior (and mainly the parents' recollection and description of behavior) and responsiveness to medications and treatment.

Mental health professionals use a book called *DSM* or *Diagnostic and Statistical Manual of Mental Disorders* (written by the American Psychiatric Association) to make diagnoses. The *DSM* provides very specific criteria for diagnosing each type of disorder. However, even though the *DSM* provides the specific criteria for diagnosing mental disorders, the various factors that go into qualifying for each of the criteria are often much more

---

Quick Definitions

Following are some brief definitions to help you understand some of the key terms related to the diagnosis of Bipolar Disorder.

Diagnosis: A term used by a professional to describe a set of particular symptoms.

Diagnostic criteria: A specific list of symptoms required for a diagnosis of a particular disorder.

Mania: An excessively intense enthusiasm, interest, or desire with irritability, many rapidly changing ideas, exaggerated pleasure, or extreme physical activity.

Depression: A condition characterized by an inability to concentrate, severe changes in sleep patterns, decreased energy, physical discomfort, irritability, and feelings of extreme sadness, dejection, and hopelessness.

Dysphoria (also described as **"mixed state"**): A condition characterized by depression and mania that either occur together or quickly and frequently alternate back and forth.

Cycle: A period of time during which someone fluctuates between different mental states.

Also see the Glossary for additional terms and definitions that relate to Bipolar Disorder.

complicated than they seem. Many of them also tend to overlap the symptoms of other disorders. It takes a professional to accurately make a diagnosis.

When most people think of Bipolar Disorder (formerly called Manic Depression), they think of alternating episodes of mania and depression with distinct differences between the types of moods. A common problem in diagnosing young children with Bipolar Disorder, however, is that the difference in their behavior during their manic periods and their depressed periods is not as clear cut as those often seen in adults. Most children with Bipolar Disorder actually have dysphoria, or mixed state periods when they experience mania and depression alternating very quickly or occuring at the same time. So, while adults' moods tend to stay in one or the other extreme for much longer, young children may swing from one end of the spectrum to the other at a very fast rate. They can cycle many times during a day. In fact, because children tend to swing from mania to depression so rapidly and frequently, it can be very difficult to tell the difference.

Furthermore, the symptoms that indicate Bipolar Disorder usually look very different in children than in adults. For example, a manic adult can jump on a plane, disappear for a few days, and/or go on a massive shopping spree. It's easy to tell that adult is being manic. Their behavior is what we typically think of as mania. Instead, a child's mania may show up as restlessness, hyperactivity, or extreme irritability.

Consequently, there is currently a lot of controversy surrounding the diagnosis of Bipolar Disorder in children. Until recently, it was commonly believed that the onset of Bipolar Disorder was, at the earliest, during adolescence or early adulthood. There are many who would still argue this case. Most medical and mental health professionals agree that the diagnostic criteria used to diagnosis Bipolar Disorder in adults don't apply to children, yet many mental health professionals are making the diagnosis in children. Even the National Institute of Mental Health, which is part of the National Institute of Health, is sponsoring research and symposiums on Bipolar Disorder in young children. Other studies by mental health professionals are researching how what is currently being called Bipolar Disorder in children might be a combination of other disorders or another type of mood disorder all together.

While some of the behaviors listed in Chapter Two may not technically be symptoms of Bipolar Disorder according to the formal diagnostic criteria that are currently used by the mental health community, they are often found in children who are later diagnosed with Bipolar Disorder, so we chose to include them. In fact, some who study the disorder have suggested that certain behaviors may not actually be symptoms of Bipolar Disorder at all, but may be personality traits that develop in children who are coping with this disorder rather than focusing on typical emotional and psychological development. Many can also be symptoms of other psychodevelopmental disorders, such as Oppositional Defiant Disorder, or of learning disabilities, such as Attention Deficit Hyperactivity Disorder. (Please see Chapter Four for more information on other disorders and their symptoms and likelihood of occurring along with Bipolar Disorder.) However, whether behaviors such as extreme irritability, difficulty in the morning, trouble with empathy, or problems with peers, for example, are actual symptoms of mental illness or consequential personality traits, they are still behaviors that need to be addressed. They are serious enough to justify exploring whether your child has a diagnosable condition, and these behaviors can be used to help the doctor make a diagnosis.

Regardless of how childhood-onset Bipolar Disorder is diagnosed or labeled in the future, we agree with the experts and with the thousands and thousands of parents whose children display these types of behaviors and are later diagnosed with Bipolar Disorder—something is going on. That "something" needs to be recognized and treated.

Now you can see why it's so important to choose a good doctor. The doctor must understand the complexities of childhood-onset Bipolar Disorder and its differences from the traditional concept of Bipolar Disorder in order to come to an accurate conclusion.

GETTING THE FORMAL DIAGNOSIS

One day it happens. A doctor you trust looks you in the eye and tells you that your child has Bipolar Disorder.

♥ *I clearly remember the day Julie was diagnosed with Bipolar Disorder. I can tell you the exact color and texture of the psychiatrist's couch. I was studying it intensely, I assume, in an effort to buffer myself from what was happening. This sounds really weird, but the only other time I had heard about this disorder was on a TV interview with Robin Givens and Mike*

Tyson. She was talking about his incredible mood swings, his temper and his abusive behaviors. He was just sitting there with this complicated look in his eyes. I couldn't tell if he was drugged or if he was planning to beat the crap out of her after the show. This was the picture that came to mind that day, in that office, on that couch. I realize now that I was trying desperately to minimize what was happening. I wanted to make it about someone else. It was too big and I felt as if I might choke.

This picture of black hearts was one of Julie's more positive drawings before she was diagnosed and treated.

Remember, a diagnosis is not an answer—it's a place to start. It does not tell us what to do. It gives us an idea of where to begin. It doesn't tell us anything more about that child than we already know. It does give us a history of other children with similar symptoms and what may or may not have worked for them. It is not an excuse for your child's behavior or a definitive answer for everything that is wrong, it is a tool to help you help your child. There may be times that the diagnosis seems perfect and times when it doesn't seem quite right. Hopefully, the time will come when you realize that as long as your child's needs are being met, it doesn't really matter what anyone wants to call it.

The diagnosis itself can be as big or as small as you choose to make it. If you keep it in the proper perspective, it will only be a positive thing for you and your child. There will be times you may have to teach others what a diagnosis is and is not. If you are comfortable and confident, your attitude will likely be contagious.

IF IT'S NOT BIPOLAR DISORDER

If you get a diagnosis, but it's not Bipolar Disorder, you can still keep reading this book. Most of the parenting techniques, tips on dealing with mental healthcare providers and insurance companies, and descriptions of the feelings that you might experience as you deal with the diagnosis and its effects on your child, yourself and your family will still apply. Just make sure you obtain additional information on the specific characteristics of and treatments for the particular mental illness that your child has. Also keep in mind that many children are given other diagnoses prior to receiving the diagnosis of Bipolar Disorder.

4

The Possibility of More Than One Diagnosis

WHEN BIPOLAR DISORDER ISN'T ALL THAT'S GOING ON

Once you finally get a diagnosis of Bipolar Disorder, it doesn't necessarily mean that you're completely done with the diagnostic process. If the diagnosis doesn't seem totally right or complete, it's important for you to keep looking for answers. It is not unusual for a child with Bipolar Disorder to be diagnosed with or show symptoms of other neurobiological disorders. In fact, Bipolar Disorder in children is almost always preceded and/or accompanied by another disorder. The "co-morbidity" rate (when a disorder co-occurs with one or more other disorders) is very high overall and extremely high with certain disorders. Don't worry, though. The term "co-morbidity" has nothing to do with death, even though it sounds like it might.

For example, according to a 2001 report from the National Institute of Mental Health, 90% of children who have onset of Bipolar Disorder prior to puberty also have ADHD. Also according to that report, 40% of children with Bipolar Disorder also meet the criteria for the diagnosis of Conduct Disorder. Ninety percent also meet the criteria for the diagnosis of Oppositional Defiant Disorder, and 60% have Obsessive Compulsive Disorder or Anxiety Disorder. Other recent studies, including one by Dr.

Demitri Papolos, the co-author of *The Bipolar Child,* suggest the co-morbidity rates of Bipolar Disorder with ADHD and with Oppositional Defiant Disorder are over 95%.

A child who will eventually be diagnosed with Bipolar Disorder will most likely have symptoms of another disorder earlier in life. Even if another disorder isn't formally diagnosed, some of your child's behavior may fall outside the lines of "normal," but not be directly attributable to Bipolar Disorder. Therefore, in addition to learning about Bipolar Disorder, you also need to explore other conditions that could possibly be contributing to your child's behavioral and emotional problems. As difficult as it is to keep adding diagnoses, rather than narrowing down the problem to one specific disorder, try not to think of it as having more problems to solve. There may be more than one cause of the symptoms, but everything is still part of this one, very important child.

♥ *The first diagnosis Julie had was Oppositional Defiant Disorder. That was when she was 5. I remember the doctor showing us the definition in a book. I couldn't believe there was an actual diagnosis for being a brat! It was such a relief to think that maybe this wasn't because of my parenting skills. By the same token, I had no idea what it meant to have this diagnosis or what to do about it. There was definitely a feeling of relief and hope knowing that there was a name and we weren't alone. The ODD definition explained some of her behavior but definitely didn't cover it all. Next we moved on to Attention Deficit Disorder. Between the two diagnoses, we were getting closer. Eventually we were given the Bipolar Disorder diagnosis and things really started to make sense. I was devastated, but it fit.*

CONDITIONS COMMONLY FOUND ALONG WITH BIPOLAR DISORDER

Following are descriptions, based on *DSM-IV* diagnostic criteria, of other disorders that are often seen in children with Bipolar Disorder. Some people would argue that the symptoms of these other disorders could just be part of Bipolar Disorder. However, it could be more than just Bipolar Disorder if your child is exhibiting several symptoms within a certain category. You and the doctor should investigate that disorder as well. As the statistics in the previous section show, very few children with Bipolar Disorder have only Bipolar Disorder.

*I felt that figuring out all the pieces of what was going on with Julie
was like putting together a puzzle. One day she left me this note. It
broke my heart, but it told me so much about how she was feeling. Her
brother Sam is drawn whole and happily saying, "Ya!" She is broken
and needs me to help put her together.*

Attention Deficit/Hyperactivity Disorder

Also known as ADD or ADHD, this disorder has become very well known
in the last few years. It has a reputation of being over-diagnosed and has
received a lot of press, mostly unfavorable. Those who have never had
direct personal experience with it may think it doesn't really exist, but
those who have know it's a very real and extremely frustrating, difficult,
and heartbreaking disability for both the child and the parents. While
there may be children who have been inaccurately diagnosed with
ADHD, there are also many children with the disorder who have not been
diagnosed at all.

ADHD frequently occurs with other disorders, and its symptoms
overlap with many other learning and behavioral disorders which, in

part, explains the large number of diagnoses. It also is a starting place for children who may later develop or be diagnosed with a more severe disorder. Remember, if your child has the onset of Bipolar Disorder before hitting puberty, she has an extremely high chance of also having ADHD.

The following are some of the possible symptoms of Attention Deficit/Hyperactivity Disorder according to the *DSM-IV*:

▲ Difficulty sustaining attention in tasks or play activities

▲ Avoids, dislikes, or is reluctant to engage in activities that require sustained mental effort

▲ Difficulty organizing tasks and activities

▲ Often loses things necessary for tasks or activities (e.g. toys, school assignments, pencils, books, etc.)

▲ Easily distracted by extraneous stimuli

▲ Fidgets with hands or feet

▲ Squirms or has difficulty remaining in seat

▲ Runs about or climbs excessively in situations in which it is inappropriate

▲ "On the go" or acts as if "driven by a motor"

▲ Talks excessively

▲ Impulsive (e.g. difficulty awaiting turn, interrupts or intrudes on others, blurts out answers before questions have been completed)

It's easy to see how some of the symptoms of Bipolar Disorder and the symptoms of ADHD could seem almost the same. Children with ADHD often have similar problems as children with Bipolar Disorder. Misbehavior, intense anger, tantrums, moodiness, and learning problems are signs of both disorders. The difference is in the nature, intensity, and tone of the symptoms. With ADHD, for example the child may have a temper tantrum that involves a lot of energy and frustration. A Bipolar child could maintain a rage with a high level of energy and intense anger for hours. A child with ADHD may have trouble in school because he can't pay attention. The Bipolar child just isn't motivated to do well. Much of an ADHD child's misbehavior happens randomly and almost by accident. It doesn't seem directed at getting someone mad on purpose. The Bipolar child looks for trouble. He picks fights, challenges authority and is highly confrontational. While the ADHD child might not be aware of certain dangers, the Bipolar child may actually seek danger. With ADHD, a child's behavior stays fairly consistent. With Bipolar Disorder, a child's behavior will fluctuate dramatically day to day and even hour to hour. Age at onset is an important criterion to discriminate between ADHD and Bipolar Disorder. According to the *DSM-IV*, ADHD begins before seven years of age. If the symptoms only show up after your child is eight years old, they may be symptoms of Bipolar Disorder.

As important as it is to understand the differences between Bipolar Disorder and ADHD, it's also important to remember how often these two disorders occur together. The age of onset of one versus the other and the difference in the symptoms of the two disorders may not be recognizable if your child has both. So, you may not be able to tell when one or the other started and which symptoms are which. You'll have to treat them both. The good news is that when you effectively treat Bipolar Disorder, many of the ADHD symptoms may disappear or become less severe.

Oppositional Defiant Disorder

As you will see from the following *DSM-IV* list, the symptoms of Oppositional Defiant Disorder (ODD) significantly overlap some of the symptoms of Bipolar Disorder. It could be argued that ODD is part of Bipolar Disorder as well as a stand-alone disorder.

▲ Often loses temper

▲ Often argues with adults

▲ Actively defies or refuses to comply with adults' requests or rules

▲ Deliberately annoys people

▲ Blames others for his or her mistakes or misbehavior

▲ Touchy or easily annoyed by others

▲ Often angry and resentful

▲ Often spiteful or vindictive

Conduct Disorder

Conduct Disorder is a more serious behavioral disorder involving violation or threatening of others' basic rights. There is a continuum of severity of this disorder ranging from mild to severe (e.g. lying and truancy to stealing, use of a weapon, or physical cruelty to others).

▲ Often bullies, threatens, or intimidates others

▲ Often initiates physical fights

▲ Physically cruel to people or animals

▲ Deliberately destroys others' property

▲ Lies to obtain goods or favors or to avoid obligations

▲ Steals

▲ Stays out at night or runs away from home

▲ Often truant from school

▲ Often violates rules

Sensory Integration Dysfunction

Sensory Integration Dysfunction is a disorder in which a person is over or under sensitive to sensory information. It is becoming much more widely understood and identified. It causes discomfort that can range from mild to very uncomfortable, even painful. This disorder can cause significant impairment at home, at school, or in social situations because it distracts the person from other, more important thoughts or activities. It can severely affect a person's quality of life. Many children with Bipolar Disorder experience symptoms of Sensory Integration Dysfunction.

▲ Over or under sensitive to touch, sounds, and/or smells

▲ Picky about clothing (e.g. tags must be removed, bothered by seams, long sleeves or new clothes)

▲ Dislikes being touched

▲ Dislikes having face washed, hair combed, nails cut, etc.

▲ Dislikes getting dirty or wet

▲ Dislikes being barefoot

▲ Talks loudly

▲ Misses parts of conversations or sounds

▲ Dislikes crowds

▲ Often covers ears with hands

▲ Picky about eating, especially about texture and/or temperature of the food

▲ Likes to hug or be hugged very tightly

▲ Plays too rough

▲ Overly sensitive to light

Obsessive Compulsive Disorder

A number of children with Bipolar Disorder will suffer from Obsessive Compulsive Disorder (OCD). It involves severe anxiety and discomfort that result in repetitive actions and/or obsessive thoughts that are an attempt to gain a sense of safety and control. It can be very time consuming and can seriously interfere with a child's relationships and daily activities.

▲ Repeated and persistent thoughts, feelings or urges that are inappropriate, intrusive and cause extreme anxiety or distress. (e.g. extreme concern about germs, constant worry about danger and harm)

"I couldn't believe it when Joey described his worries to his psychiatrist. He constantly worried about the walls of his room caving in on him and about

Joey's illustration of his obsessive worries about bridges falling.

Joey's illustrations of his obsessive worries about walls caving in.

car crashes and bridges falling down on us when we're in the car. He said that he knew the worries were silly and weren't really going to happen, but he still couldn't stop thinking about them." (Sheryl)

▲ Repetitive behaviors or mental acts that are done obsessively and according to a rigid set of rules, (e.g. hand washing, lining up toys in a precise order, counting, flicking lights on and off a certain number of times, etc.)

Generalized Anxiety Disorder

Anxiety is defined as a state of uneasiness or apprehension. Some level of anxiety is normal and experienced by all human beings. Children with Generalized Anxiety Disorder, however, experience frequent or almost constant intense apprehension, anticipation, fear or uncertainty. The anxiety is so intense, in fact, that it disrupts their ability to function normally. When looking at the following diagnostic criteria, make sure to keep intensity in mind.

▲ Excessive anxiety and worry about events or activities to the point that the thoughts impair the child's ability to function

▲ Anxiety and worry along with one or more of the following symptoms:

    ▲ Restlessness or feeling keyed up or on edge

    ▲ Easily fatigued

    ▲ Difficulty concentrating or mind going blank

    ▲ Irritability

    ▲ Muscle tension

    ▲ Sleep disturbance

Panic Disorder

According to the *DSM-IV*, Panic Disorder is a characterized by "panic attacks" that are unpredictable and seem to come out of nowhere since they don't seem to be directly connected with a specific traumatic event or situation. A panic attack consists of a feeling of intense, sudden terror or fear and extreme discomfort with a sense of impending doom. Panic attacks can happen several times a week or even several times per day. They reach their peak in about 10 minutes and, after they're gone, leave the individual emotionally drained and frightened. The physical sensations during a panic attack may include:

▲ Racing, pounding heartbeat and chest pain that may seem similar to a heart attack

▲ Breathlessness, choking sensation

▲ Flushes or chills

▲ Sweating

▲ Trembling, tingling or numbness

▲ Feelings of hopelessness or loss of control

Other problems that occur with Panic Disorder include panic-related phobias and feelings of poor overall well-being.

Tic Disorder or Tourette's Syndrome

Many children with Bipolar Disorder will have some sort of tic disorder at one time or another. A tic is described as an involuntary, sudden muscular movement, contraction or vocalization. Some examples of tics would be eye blinking, facial grimaces, lip licking, throat clearing, yelling or repetitive sounds. The tics can occur many times in a day and can be very distressing and embarrassing. The good news is that, in a lot of cases, these tics will disappear by the age of 18. There are three types of tic disorders:

▲ Transient Tic Disorder: Single or multiple motor and/or vocal tics that occur during a period of more than 4 weeks and less than 1 year

▲ Chronic Tic Disorder: Single or multiple motor or vocal tics (not both) lasting more than one year without having a tic-free period lasting more than 3 consecutive months

▲ Tourette's Syndrome (also called Tourette's Disorder): Both motor and one or more vocal tics lasting more than 1 year without having a tic-free episode lasting more than 3 consecutive months

Asperger's Syndrome

Asperger's Syndrome is a disorder many may not be familiar with. It is considered a social disability and is an Autistic Spectrum Disorder. The term "high functioning autism" is sometimes used interchangeably with Asperger's Syndrome. The *DSM-IV* lists its symptoms as:

▲ Impairment in social interaction

▲ Difficulty in using or failure to use several different nonverbal behaviors such as eye contact, facial expression, and gestures involved in social interaction (e.g. doesn't wave goodbye, doesn't show emotion through facial expression)

▲ Failure to develop developmentally-appropriate peer relationships

▲ Doesn't spontaneously seek to share enjoyment, interests, or achievements with other people (e.g. doesn't show, bring, or point out objects of interest)

▲ Lack of common social interactions (e.g. doesn't share, doesn't say thank you)

▲ Restricted, repetitive, and stereotyped patterns of behavior, interests, and activities

▲ Preoccupation with one or more areas of interest in a way that is abnormal either in intensity or focus (e.g. ability to exactly repeat the script of a favorite movie, refusal to watch anything but one favorite movie or to read anything but one favorite book)

▲ Inflexible about following specific routines or rituals that don't really serve any purpose (e.g. always having to sit in a certain chair, refusal to do parts of a routine, such as getting ready for bed, out of the normal order)

▲ Repetitive physical activities (e.g. hand or finger flapping)

▲ Preoccupation with parts of objects (e.g. obsessed with the wheels of a toy car but doesn't play with the whole car)

▲ Lack of control over voice tone, expression and volume (e.g. speaking in a monotone, tending to talk too loud, tending to talk very fast or very slowly)

THE IMPORTANCE OF LOOKING AT OTHER DISORDERS

It's likely that you are feeling totally overwhelmed at this point. Now you have the possibility of not just one difficult diagnosis, but more as well. This is a great time to remind yourself why you are doing all this; you are trying to figure out what's going on with your child so you can understand him as much as possible, support him in as many ways as possible, and obtain the appropriate services and resources to help him.

It's important to identify and understand all the symptoms affecting your child because some treatments for other disorders can actually worsen the symptoms of Bipolar Disorder. One example is Ritalin, a medication commonly used to treat ADHD. Because this stimulant can increase or even bring on mania, it shouldn't be given before the child's mood has been stabilized with other medications. Once the Bipolar Disorder has been treated, though, the ADHD symptoms may improve. If they don't, they can be successfully, and usually easily, treated at this point. Anti-depressants are another example. They also can increase or bring on mania.

To make matters even more complicated, when symptoms of a secondary disorder, such as ADHD seem to be getting worse, it may actually be that the Bipolar Disorder isn't under control. Modifying the treatment for Bipolar Disorder can help improve the child's attention span when an increase in Ritalin may not. You can see how important it is to know everything you're dealing with.

"The first diagnosis for Jamie was ADHD. The psychiatrist told us to be more consistent in our discipline and put him on Ritalin, which seemed to make him worse. After the dosage was increased several times, he went from being manic to having bizarre hallucinations. Then a different specialist told us that he had Oppositional Defiant Disorder and Anxiety Disorder. After many medication changes, special school programs, assessments and recommendations (he even had an MRI to rule out organic causes for his behavioral and emotional problems), we finally found a psychiatrist who thought that Jamie might have Bipolar Disorder. He eventually was diagnosed with Bipolar as well as Obsessive Compulsive Disorder when he was 7. The whole process took almost two years. The good news is that once we had the complete diagnoses and he was put on the right combination of medications, he got much better." (Bob)

Remember, whether you prefer to look at it as your child actually having another disorder, having symptoms of another disorder, or all the symptoms being part of one disorder, the symptoms need to be treated. They are a significant, unpleasant aspect of your child's life that probably can be improved. Only by recognizing the symptoms and taking the steps to treat them can you truly help your child. If you only are open to addressing the "Bipolar symptoms," you limit how far you can go to help your child. If you treat the other symptoms without taking the Bipolar Disorder into consideration, you could make matters worse.

Adjusting to the Bipolar Diagnosis

5

Your Feelings About the Diagnosis

HAVING THE "ANSWER"

You may breathe a huge sigh of relief once you know that your child's behavioral problems have a biological or chemical cause; it's not just that he's being bad or that you're unable to control him. You may also feel the thrill of being able to say, "I told you so. I knew something was wrong." This can be an empowering time, you feel like you might finally have some answers. You have options that you can try in order to help your child. You have people who believe what you're saying about your child. What's more, you know that you're not alone.

According to the U.S. Surgeon General's 12/14/99 report on mental health:

▲ 22% of the population has a diagnosable mental disorder

▲ Mental illness is the 2nd leading cause of disability in the country

▲ 1 in 5 children experiences signs and symptoms of a diagnosable mental disorder during the course of a year

▲ 5% of children suffer extreme functional impairment from a mental disorder

Based on these figures, this means up to 14 million children in the United States suffer from a diagnosable neurobiological disorder.

At some point, however, it will suddenly hit you that your child has a mental disorder. You may have visions of your child as the stereotypical mentally ill person locked in a ward of raving lunatics or wandering dirty and hungry on the streets. Your feelings may fluctuate from being empowered to wanting to cry. Now you have a whole new set of worries and issues to deal with that are so significant, they can make you wish the problem really is that you're a lousy parent!

All the fluctuations you're feeling may leave you wondering whether or not you're the one with the mood disorder. Whether you feel like bombarding yourself with information or going to bed and pulling the covers over your head, you're on the road to helping your child at last. It may not feel like it at this point, but having a diagnosis (or diagnoses, as the case may be) is a good thing, not a bad thing.

♥ *After a few days of processing the Bipolar diagnosis, I began to feel stronger in one sense, but overwhelmed in another. I felt like I had climbed up a huge mountain and when I got high enough to see what was on the other side, there was another mountain, this one even taller and steeper than the first.*

YOUR FEELINGS ABOUT YOUR CHILD

Now that you know your child has Bipolar Disorder, a whole new set of emotions is likely to arise, not just about the disorder, but also about your child. Suddenly, you look at her in a new light. No longer is the behavior problem a separate thing to be addressed and solved so that your child is cured. The problem, you now know, is part of your child's brain. It can be treated, but it won't go away.

Throughout this book, we have used the term "Bipolar child" because we've decided to take the approach that Bipolar Disorder is an integral part of the child. Just because we have a name that describes the reasons behind her behavior and emotions, doesn't mean that we can separate it from who she is. This approach is our choice, but you might be more comfortable thinking of your child as a "child with Bipolar Disorder." The difference might sound slight, but thinking about how you personally choose to approach your child now that you have the Bipolar diagnosis can help you manage the intense feelings that we all encounter. It doesn't matter whether you think of Bipolar Disorder as affecting your child or actually being a part of who she is. What is important is to treat your child and the disorder as being continuously and irreversibly connected. You can't treat one without considering the other.

> *"I struggle with the idea that if we could just make Arielle's symptoms go away we could find out how she normally would be. I keep looking for the child that I thought I would have. What I keep reminding myself is that the Bipolar Disorder affects her thinking process and her moods, not just her behavior. To a large degree, her personality is caught up in it. There is no 'Arielle without Bipolar.' It is a part of her. To wish the Bipolar away is almost to wish away many of the special aspects of my child."* (Claire)

> *"I think about Brianne having a disease like diabetes. It's not something that can go away. It can just be treated. It's just the way her body functions."* (Connie)

> *"At times I find myself hating the Bipolar Disorder. I feel like it has attacked my child. I want it to go away and leave him alone."* (Amy)

> *"I have a whole new respect for Daniel now that I know what he's dealing with. I'm amazed at how much effort he has to put into every aspect of his life. He's an incredibly strong person to be willing to keep working at improving his behavior."* (Denise)

It's easy to wish that our children were "normal." Sure, it sounds much simpler to parent a "normal" child. Consider the definition of normal: standard, common, typical or average. Is this really what you want your child to be? What she is might be hard for you to cope with, and certainly you wish that life could be easier for both of you, but she has amazing potential and unlimited possibilities because of her differences from "normal."

Different doesn't always mean bad. There are many positive aspects of Bipolar Disorder. Intellectual giftedness, high energy level, passion, and extraordinary creativity are characteristics that are often found in those with Bipolar Disorder. The passion and intensity Bipolar people possess can be incredibly productive.

What Does Your Child Have in Common With The Following Artists, Actors, Writers and Musicians?

Hans Christian Anderson

Many great poets, including Byron, Shelley, Keats

Vincent Van Gogh

Edgar Allan Poe

F. Scott Fitzgerald

Tchaikovsky

Tennessee Williams

Cole Porter

Georgia O'Keefe

Charles Dickens

Emily Dickenson

T.S. Eliot

All these accomplished people were known to have serious, sometimes debilitating moodiness and emotional fluctuations. Many wrote about the intense thoughts that raced through their minds. Many were in psychiatric hospitals at some point in their lives. Some attributed their creative abilities to the intense emotions they experienced. Based on historical records of their behavior, it's highly likely that if they were being assessed today, they would be diagnosed with a mood disorder such as Bipolar Disorder.

There are many other historical examples of "mad geniuses" and "crazy artists." Keep in mind these famous people who have had Bipolar Disorder or other mood disorders and the wonderful things they've done. They didn't fit the mold of a "normal" person. The behaviors they had that were "bad" or "different" are partly what enabled them to do the wonderful, creative things they did that changed the world. The very symptoms that define the most difficult aspects of Bipolar Disorder are some of same ones that have served as a catalyst to some of the world's greatest art, music and literature.

Accompanying these wonderful qualities are also other symptoms that can lead to socially unacceptable and even dangerous behavior; so, while it's important to recognize that there are some benefits to Bipolar Disorder, it still needs to be managed. Although you may regret the many challenges that your child will face in her life and at times wish that you could know who she would have been if she didn't have Bipolar Disorder, at least you can know that she has incredible potential, if her symptoms are managed. What's more, she will always be different, interesting and dynamic and a far cry from normal and ordinary. It may not be an easy path, but it can be an incredible journey.

"One of the best things about my daughter is the incredible flashes of insight she has. She is more aware of and interested in the world around her than most adults. She doesn't take anything for granted and questions almost everything. She not only gathers information, but she integrates it to figure out how things are interrelated. Sure, I wish she could channel some of that intellectual curiosity into her schoolwork, but Einstein didn't do so well at school, either. School isn't everything. I think she's got the potential to change the world! We just have to let her do it in her own way." (Kim)

"Whenever I get depressed about how difficult some of the normal aspects of life are for Byron, I look back at his baby book. He has always been so precocious. That counts for a lot." (Monica)

"Michael may not be able to get an A on a test, or even focus on the test long enough to get a B, but he can discuss all the concepts with any adult. I have to remember not to judge his knowledge or abilities just by the grades he gets in school." (Brian)

EDUCATING YOURSELF

Now that you've gotten the diagnosis and have had a little while to let it sink in, you may be glad to have an "answer," but you probably also have more questions. You're probably saying "What now?" or "How do I fix it?" This means that you need even more information. It's time to shift the focus from "what is it?" to "how do you deal with it?"

Addressing Bipolar Disorder is a process that takes a lot of patience, on-going observation and a constantly changing array of parenting techniques. It also takes a lot of education to understand not just the symptoms of Bipolar Disorder, but also all the options that are available to treat it. In addition to reading this book, which will help make it easier to live with and love your Bipolar child, it's also important to understand the medical and clinical aspects of the disorder.

Start by expanding your home library to include books that specifically focus on the disorder and its treatment. There's also a lot of information on the Internet. The National Association of the Mentally Ill and The National Institute of Mental Health, for example, both have very informative websites. (We've included suggested books and website addresses in the *Additional Resources* section.) Ask your mental health professional for suggestions on reading material and support groups. These books and resources will help you begin to learn more about Bipolar Disorder and how to help your child.

Get connected with other parents of Bipolar children, too. Like the information in this book, their input will help you understand how having a Bipolar child affects your life. They will make you feel supported when it feels like no one else understands what you're dealing with. These parents can recommend schools and doctors, share books, offer suggestions on parenting techniques or childcare, as well as provide a wealth of other important information that will help you help yourself and your child. Contact your child's school, local religious organizations, and local chapters of mental health associations to find out about support groups and resources for parents of special needs kids. Check out websites and chatrooms online; just type in "bipolar child" in the search engines.

6

Other People's Reactions to the Diagnosis

WAYS TO EXPLAIN MENTAL ILLNESS

The brain is the most complex system in the human body. Is it really any surprise that things can and do go wrong? When the brain has a problem, the problem affects the two things that the brain controls: physical functions and mental thought. People seem to have an easy time understanding when a brain problem affects how the body works, such as when a person with Parkinson's shakes or a person with epilepsy has a seizure. They don't quite understand when a brain problem has an uncontrollable, negative effect on how a person thinks, behaves or feels.

Here are a few important thoughts to help you to explain and understand Bipolar Disorder or mental illness in general. Hopefully these concepts will help you put it into perspective and reassure yourself, as well as others.

▲ Bipolar Disorder is a biologically-based disorder just like diabetes. Both are caused by chemical imbalances. One happens in the brain, the other in the pancreas. Bipolar Disorder shouldn't be thought of or treated any differently than any other type of physical disorder.

▲ The brain is a part of the body. It can be affected by disorders that

62

can't be seen or easily understood, just as any other part of the body can.

▲ The effects of Bipolar Disorder can be compared to a brain tumor or Alzheimer's. Both directly affect behavior and can vary in intensity at different times, for no apparent reason. You wouldn't hold the outbursts of an old man with Alzheimer's against him. He can't control them. So why would we hold a Bipolar child's outbursts against her? We must not expect that the child's behaviors can be changed by choice or willpower.

▲ We must learn to treat those affected by any mental disorder with the same care and compassion we give to those dealing with any other physical problem.

▲ We must also acknowledge, accept, and deal with the effects the disease has on the child and everyone around her. We can do this for people whose lives are turned upside down by a physical illness such as cancer, why can't we do it for someone with a mental illness?

TELLING PEOPLE ABOUT THE DIAGNOSIS

When you begin to share your child's diagnosis with other people you will likely learn that dealing with a diagnosis of any type of mental illness isn't like dealing with a diagnosis of diabetes or cancer. Prepare yourself for a wide variety of reactions, even from the people who love you and your child the most. Usually, parents of a sick child get lots of support when they share the news with others. People tend to be sympathetic and want to be helpful. That's not typically the case when a child's diagnosis is a mental illness. Instead, some people may respond in a critical and judgmental, and even fearful way. People may offer you lots of parenting advice, as if something you did or didn't do caused the problem. They might even try to step in and attempt to solve the problem themselves. Other people will minimize it, saying that all children just act that way. Even well-intentioned family and friends may inadvertently say things that hurt. Instead of freely sharing your thoughts and feelings about your child's problems, you may end up feeling embarrassed and ashamed, as if you could have prevented it or it is somehow a reflection of your parenting.

"I once told a neighbor about my struggles with Patrick. She said there was nothing wrong with him that a good spanking wouldn't fix. I tried to explain about Bipolar Disorder but she just rolled her eyes. People can be so clueless. I won't make that mistake again." (Colleen)

Our society has a long history of supporting the idea that mental illness is something to be ashamed of. People expect that we should be able to control our behavior and that our moods should, for the most part, be kept in check. As a result, most people are extremely uneducated about mental illness, especially in children. Some people don't even believe in psychiatry in general.

"There is so much controversy over ADHD and whether or not it is real, used as an excuse and over-diagnosed that I think many people are reluctant to accept any type of psychiatric or brain chemistry problem in children— especially if it requires medication." (Caroline)

Most people expect children to learn to be in control of their behavior. Our children are not able to do this on their own or even with our help. This is very hard for outsiders to understand and even harder to accept. It's easier to find a way to blame the parents than to believe that things like this happen to children and families.

♥ *It is so important to protect yourself and your child from people who cannot or will not understand and support you. You can't educate people who don't want to be educated. You cannot expect people to accept your child if they are intolerant. You must be prepared for the criticism of others. A lot of people will find ways to blame you for your child's problems. You're too strict . . . you're not strict enough . . . you don't spend enough time with your child . . . give me one day with her and I'd whip her right into shape . . . if you just did x, y, and z, she'd be fine . . . she just needs a little structure . . . she is just a manipulative child, etc. I have heard these things far more times than I'd like to remember. It's so painful to devote your whole life to your child's well-being only to be blamed for her illness.*

All you can do is educate yourself and believe in what you are doing. You know what is right and true in your heart. Be prepared for ignorance—it is all around you. The sooner you learn how to avoid and ignore it, the less heartache and anger you will experience.

> *"A few days after my brother Jesse attempted suicide, my nephew Cody got badly mauled by a full-grown black bear. Even though I've become incredibly educated about Bipolar Disorder, my first instinct was to think of Cody's life-threatening situation as more 'real' than Jesse's, even though both had almost just lost their lives and both were in the hospital. It's just so much easier to understand the physical damage than the mental damage. I felt guilty for feeling this way, but I guess it's a natural response. It seems like Cody had an accident happen to him and that Jesse did something that we wish he could have controlled. In reality, though, Jesse really couldn't control the voices in his head any more than Cody could control the bear."* (Sheryl)

Remember that your priority isn't telling other people in order to help them. Your focus should be on telling people who can help you and/or your child. If someone doesn't really need to know, you're not obligated to tell him/her. The only reason to share the diagnosis with anyone at this point is if it will benefit you or your child. Different people have different opinions and comfort levels on sharing personal information. Do whatever feels good to you and expect that how you feel about it won't always stay the same. Accept that you will make mistakes. There will likely be times when you tell someone and later wish you hadn't and other times you finally tell someone and wish you had told them much sooner. Being a parent is "on the job training." Your instincts will only get better over time and with experience.

> ♥ *I used to feel it was important for me to educate people about Bipolar Disorder, but now I know how critical it is not to do that at the expense of my child's reputation and acceptance in the community. It is too easy for your child to then become the official scapegoat for any problems that may arise. I am definitely not saying to keep Bipolar Disorder a secret or not to educate and inform others, I am saying that it is so important to be careful how and with whom you do it.*

> *"My friend was at a board meeting for a private school. One board member was advocating that the school publish a list of all children who are taking or*

have taken psychiatric medication. Her rationale was that there is a connection between these drugs and school violence. How scary is that?" (Melissa)

"I tell people on a need-to-know basis. Just my family, a few close friends and the school know about Jeremy's diagnosis. I'm afraid other people will just put a label on my child and be judgmental of me. I feel I am protecting him by telling as few people as possible. He has so many struggles already, I don't want him to have to deal with other people knowing he has medical diagnoses as well." (Karen)

"I'm a pretty open person. I tend to talk a lot about what's going on in my life, so I'm certainly not going to hold back on sharing information that is as important as Bipolar Disorder. I'm thrilled to finally know what's going on. I want to share the information with other people so they know that Samantha has a real reason for her behavior. If they can't handle the truth, that's their problem, not mine." (Jane)

"Our parents are obsessed with figuring out where the Bipolar Disorder came from. I guess it's good that they understand that it's biological and has some hereditary aspects, but I wish they were less focused on placing blame and more focused on understanding how it affects their grandchild and us, their children." (Dayna)

"When Zachary shows his most extreme behavior in public, I just tell salesclerks, waiters and other people that my son is 'special.' They don't need to know the whole story, but I do want them to know that I'm not just allowing or encouraging that type of behavior. When I took Zach to get a haircut, for example, he went crazy because the chair was green. He went on and on about how he did not want to sit in a green chair. I just smiled and said, 'He's special!' When a barber was trying to make friends with Zach and kept asking him questions, which Zach completely ignored, I just casually suggested that he talk to my younger child instead." (Adrienne)

Hopefully, many of your friends and family members will be understanding and supportive and want to help. One of the easiest ways people can help you is to educate themselves. Encourage them to read books and do research on the Internet. Ask them to research a particular topic for you. They can help you, feel empowered and get educated at the same time. The more people you and your child have on your "team," the better. (Please see Chapter 10 for suggestions on managing the effects of Bipolar Disorder on your extended family and on your social life.)

"Playgroup was when Cindy, Sherri, Heidi and I watched and discussed our kids' progress as they grew from toddlers to preschoolers. I don't know how Cindy stood it. Early on, as our kids were exerting their independence and trying to do things on their own, Julie was practically attached to Cindy's leg. She didn't want to be held, she just wanted to hold onto Cindy. Later, while Julie was the first to really be able to keep her Pull-Ups dry and use the potty, she was also the one who would just pee on the floor for no reason. We talked about starting to use time-outs when our kids threw temper tantrums. Cindy, I found out later, sometimes locked Julie in her room to stop her from hurting herself during hours of rages. Julie was clearly more physically coordinated than the other kids. She was also much more verbal. We were all so impressed with her, even though she was often at the center of arguments and physical fights among the kids. Little did we know that almost everything that characterized our descriptions of Julie were signals that something wasn't quite right. We just thought she was a difficult child. After Cindy told everyone the full story, which was quite a while after she found out, we realized that we had only been seeing a small part of what was going on. Knowing the truth made it much easier for us to help Cindy. We could discipline Julie when she got out of control, explain to our kids why they needed to give Julie a little slack about her behavior, and give Cindy a chance to talk freely in playgroup. It also made playgroup a lot more fun for everyone because there weren't any secrets, and Cindy was much more relaxed once she could stop worrying that we might hold Julie's behavior against her." (Sheryl)

TALKING TO YOUR CHILD ABOUT BIPOLAR DISORDER

Depending on the age of your child, you may also need to tell him what's going on. Remember that it doesn't matter what you call it. You can use the actual name of the disorder or just explain that it's a problem with brain chemicals, whichever you think will work best for your child.

What's important is to help him understand that there is a real reason why he has a hard time controlling his moods and thoughts and that you don't blame him for what he can't control. Discuss how medication and therapy can help his brain function better. Talk to him about how you both can work together to help him behave more appropriately.

♥ *It was important to me that Julie understood that she has a biological problem with the chemicals in her brain that affect her behavior and thoughts. Could an 8 year-old possibly understand that? I needed to come up with an analogy that she could relate to. I wanted to tell her the truth, but in terms that she could comprehend. I described to her how there are chemicals that are much like pieces of a puzzle that carry information in the brain. Certain types of messages are "shaped" in certain ways. Certain parts of the brain have the right shape for the puzzle pieces to fit. With Bipolar Disorder, her body sometimes doesn't make enough of certain types of puzzle pieces or sometimes makes the pieces the wrong shape. This means her brain can't always get all the messages it needs in order for her to stay in control of her thoughts and behavior. The medicine she takes puts the right shape puzzle pieces into her brain so it can work better.*

"When Joey was diagnosed with Obsessive Compulsive Disorder, I started to explain to him how his brain is like a computer that needs the right chemicals to carry electrical messages from one part of his brain to another. Before I could take a breath at the end of my sentence, he said, 'oh, it's like my brain has a computer virus.' I agreed, and that was all the discussion he wanted or needed. He didn't care what the name was at all." (Sheryl)

"My father doesn't like it that I talk about Carissa's Bipolar Disorder in front of her. He says that it's not an appropriate topic for a child and that we shouldn't acknowledge it. I totally disagree. I think that if we're uncomfortable talking about it within our own family, Carissa will grow up thinking it's something to be ashamed of." (Eileen)

TALKING TO YOUR OTHER CHILDREN ABOUT BIPOLAR DISORDER

Even a very young child can understand that a sibling has a problem in his brain that he can't control and that makes him behave badly sometimes. Consider each child's age and unique temperament, then develop an explanation that has the appropriate level of detail and complexity. Be 100% honest (even if you're not necessarily being 100% comprehensive) and available to answer questions. Remember that kids sometimes like information in bits and pieces when the topic arises naturally (such as when their sibling is raging), rather than a formal presentation or discussion.

If they're old enough, your other children will probably be incredibly relieved to find out that there's a real reason why their sibling behaves the way he does. They'll probably lose some of the conscious or unconscious resentment about why you end up spending so much of your time and energy on that sibling. They'll also probably worry that it might happen to them, that their sibling will always get more attention, and that their sibling might get sicker. They might end up behaving badly in order to attract more of your attention. There's a huge range of emotions that they might experience, just as you do. You'll have to support your other children, both when you first explain the diagnosis to them and as your family has ongoing experiences of life with a Bipolar child. You also have to explain to them, repeatedly, that Bipolar Disorder is a reason for much of their sibling's difficulties, but it is not an excuse for getting away with poor behavior, especially toward them. (Please see Chapter 10 for suggestions on how to take care of your other children while you're taking care of your Bipolar child.)

> *"Jordan, 11, was amazed that Joey could take pills that would help him stop worrying. When Jordan had a problem that he was upset about, he told me that he thought he should have pills, too, so he wouldn't have to be upset. I had to explain the difference between being upset about something real and having uncontrollable, unreasonable, unstoppable worries like Joey had. Thank goodness Jordan clearly couldn't even imagine feeling like that."*
> (Sheryl)

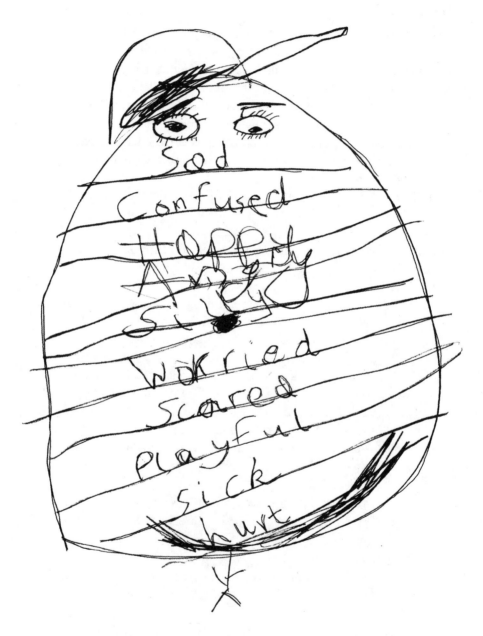

An illustration of how it feels to have Bipolar Disorder

SECTION THREE:

Helping Your Child Get Treatment

7

Coordinating Your Child's Treatment

Getting the diagnosis may feel like you've finally reached your destination, but you still have a long journey ahead of you as you get treatment for your child. After getting the diagnosis of Bipolar Disorder, your child will likely be prescribed psychiatric medication. Medication is often the first step in treatment because until your child's moods are stabilized, it is difficult to learn how to manage and understand thoughts, which are the keys to changing and gaining more control over behaviors. Therapy is another important part of treatment. While it can be tempting to want to rely on just one or the other aspect of treatment, depending on your feelings about medicating your child and having a child in regular therapy, the combination of the two has proven to be the most effective.

CREATING AND MANAGING YOUR CHILD'S MEDICAL TEAM

Bipolar Disorder is, at times, too difficult for one person, or even two parents, to handle on their own. What's more, just one doctor might not be enough either. You'll likely need a team of professionals who can help you deal with your child's complex medical and psychiatric needs. Luckily, you can use most of the same strategies you used in Chapter 3 to choose the best professionals for your child.

Your team of professionals will include some of the following. Keep in mind that your insurance may dictate which types of professionals you are able to use.

▲ **Psychiatrist:** A medical doctor who can prescribe medications, provide therapy or other treatment, and supervise any medical tests required to monitor certain psychiatric medications. This may or may not be the same psychiatrist who made the original diagnosis. You chose that doctor for his/her diagnostic skills. Now you need one who has the approach to on-going treatment that you want.

▲ **Psychologist:** A professional, who is not a medical doctor, who specializes in therapy. A psychologist may be trained and licensed specifically to provide child therapy. Psychologists may be more accessible for appointments and tend to cost less than psychiatrists. They can provide psychological testing, identify learning disorders, make a diagnosis and provide therapeutic treatment, but they cannot prescribe medication.

▲ **Therapist:** A licensed professional who has training in therapeutic techniques. These professionals may be social workers or individuals who obtained a degree or certification related to psychology. The best therapist is one who is experienced and establishes rapport with your child.

▲ **Pediatrician:** A medical doctor who monitors your child's physical health and may supervise some of the medical tests required for monitoring certain psychiatric medications. The pediatrician you use needs to see the big picture and understand all aspects of your child's health. If your current pediatrician isn't able or willing to do this or doesn't fully support the Bipolar diagnosis, find a different pediatrician.

▲ **Pharmacist:** A medical professional who has extensive knowledge of the effects and side effects of medications, their interactions with other drugs, and dosages.

▲ **School counselor:** Your child's school or school district has specialists, usually social workers or psychologists, who help coordinate special services that your child may need to help her be successful in school. Even though school counselors aren't technically healthcare professionals, it's good for the counselor to be informed of, if not involved in, your child's care. He/she has access to information about what your child does for a large portion of her day, so he/she likely can offer valuable input and referrals to other services.

Tell every single professional treating your child about her condition and medications. This is even true for the dentist, eye doctor, and any other specialist who treats your child. Full knowledge will help them make the best medical decisions for your child. For example, some psychiatric medications cause dry mouth. If your dentist knows that your child is taking that type of medication, he/she can expect a higher risk of cavities and might schedule cleaning appointments more frequently.

DEALING WITH HEALTHCARE PROFESSIONALS

When you do find healthcare professionals with whom you feel comfortable, remember that even though they are the professionals, you are the parent. You have the ultimate responsibility for your child. Therefore, you must consistently be an active participant in all decisions regarding your child's treatment. No one knows your child better than you do! Your instincts and perceptions are relevant and valid. If what a healthcare professional is telling you doesn't seem right, don't just assume that you must be wrong. Encourage him/her to give you additional explanations and to reconsider your input. If you still aren't comfortable, seek a second opinion and, if necessary, switch to a different healthcare professional. Sometimes, even if you do think a healthcare professional is on the right track, it's still a good idea to get a second opinion, especially when critical diagnoses or serious medication decisions are being made.

♥ *I've learned from experience that if I trust my instincts, I'll be correct about 99% of the time. Even if I can't logically say why I feel a certain way about a particular doctor, decision, or diagnosis, I try to listen to what my gut says. If a healthcare professional doesn't respect this, that's not the right one for me or for my child.*

When you've built an effective healthcare team for your child, you will need to serve as a liaison between the team members. Because Bipolar Disorder is a biologically-based psychodevelopmental disorder, it's going to be critical that the various professionals treating your child, including the psychiatrist, therapist, and pediatrician, communicate with each other. This shouldn't be done just as a professional courtesy, either. Your child will be on medications that affect both her mind and her body. These caregivers must share information and treat the whole child, not just the part in which they specialize. If they don't do this on their own, you must facilitate the process by setting up joint meetings, reminding them to send copies of medical and therapy records to each other, and sharing all test results and changes in your child's treatment or condition.

In addition, as your child's advocate, you have every right, in fact you have a responsibility, to fully understand everything that is going on with your child. Each time a new medication or a new approach to treatment begins, ask as many questions as necessary to help you fully understand what will be happening. If a caregiver isn't willing to provide full explanations in terms you understand and answer any questions you still might have, find a new caregiver.

GETTING THERAPY

Whether your child receives her therapy from a psychiatrist, a psychologist, a social worker, a therapist, or a combination of these types of professionals, the focus should be on helping your child learn to recognize the feelings and thoughts that cause her to behave in inappropriate or dangerous ways. It should also help her develop her own skills in stopping or redirecting those thoughts and feelings, behave in more appropriate ways, and cope with any difficult symptoms that might not go away, even with the right medication. The hope is that with her brain chemistry stabilized, she can learn to manage whatever mood fluctuations and negative feelings the medication can't completely control.

There are different methods of therapy to assist your child to learn to feel better emotionally, interact better with others, and solve problems she encounters. In most cases the therapist (we'll use this term to reflect whomever is providing the therapy, regardless of his/her credentials) will use whatever approach seems to work best with your child. Cognitive behavioral therapy is one of the most common and successful types of therapy for Bipolar Disorder. It focuses on actual, current situations and problems. This therapy addresses thoughts and feelings ("cognitive") and actions ("behavioral") and how they affect each other. Your child can learn specific skills to help her identify when she's having distorted perceptions of situations, modify her beliefs, and change to a more appropriate manner of responding in those situations. It gives the child the opportunity to discuss what's going on in her life and to learn how to change unhealthy thoughts, feelings, and behaviors.

Your child's treatment might also include play therapy, in which she'll be involved in different types of activities in order to create opportunities for addressing her frustrations, preferences, and approaches to problems. This is particularly helpful for young children who can't yet put their feelings into words. Group therapy helps kids with similar issues address social skills. Family therapy, in which the entire family gets involved in therapy sessions together can help the Bipolar child as well as the rest of the family to identify, address and improve their understanding of each other, the situations that frequently trigger problems, and their patterns of interaction. Other therapy methods may be mentioned to you or just incorporated into the therapy as it progresses.

Regardless of the type of therapy that is used for your child, you should be an integral part of the process. You should have the opportunity to provide input on goals, feedback on what does and doesn't seem to be working, and obtain information from the therapist on what progress is being made with your child. This will probably be accomplished through a combination of meetings that you hold privately with the therapist, sessions that you attend with your child, and conversations that the therapist has with you after private meetings with your child. While you should have complete access to information about your child's diagnoses, progress, issues, and treatment, you might not be told everything that your child talks about. It's important that your child feels comfortable sharing information confidentially with the therapist.

♥ *Sometimes I've felt like the doctors must have thought that I was the one with the mental problem. I would describe the horrors that go on in my house, but Julie would just sit and talk with them like a little angel.*

"*I have such a hard time with letting my son and the therapist direct the therapy toward what they think is important. I just don't trust that Nathan is telling the therapist the truth about his behaviors and worries. I hope that the therapist is skilled enough to see through Nathan's manipulativeness, but I just don't feel comfortable that anyone who doesn't actually see what goes on in our house can truly understand how Nathan is. The therapist does ask for my input regarding how things are going and what my concerns are, but I still wish I could be in the sessions with them, even though the therapist said that wouldn't be a good idea because Nathan has to feel comfortable with saying anything that he wants to say. I'm going to ask the therapist if we can meet once in a while to discuss my concerns about therapy."* (Rose)

MONITORING YOUR CHILD'S TREATMENT

As the most important member of your child's medical team, you have the enormous responsibility of monitoring your child's progress to determine what is and isn't working with both therapy and medication, and for keeping the medical professionals informed, especially when you think additional intervention is needed. Documenting your child's behaviors, moods, outbursts, sleep patterns, energy levels and other characteristics is an extremely helpful way to make this huge task easier. You can use your written records to relay information to the caregiver, identify behavior patterns, make medication decisions, or track successful behavior modification techniques.

To keep a log of your child's behaviors and moods, write notes about positive and negative behaviors, duration, time of day, parenting techniques used, how the child responded, what triggered the event, strategies that helped end the episode, sleeping habits, eating habits, etc. You also need to keep detailed notes about medications. This can be recorded in the mood log or in a separate journal. You'll need to write down all medications that your child is taking, date started, date stopped, dosage, time of day it's taken, blood test dates and results, effects, and side effects. Even if your child is only on one medication, start a log. Time passes and before you know it, you have made several changes, added something, changed a dose, changed the time the medication is given, etc. Even if it seems simple now, it can be very difficult down the road to remember all the details you'll want to recall when making future medication decisions.

This monitoring may feel like another huge responsibility that you have to add to your role as a parent, but it is definitely worth doing. Relying solely on your memory is almost impossible, especially considering the intensity level, high emotions, and complexity of your parenting experience. The type of patterns that can be identified from the information in your log may make a significant contribution to successful treatment.

Following are some examples of medication/behavior logs.

Example 1:

Oct. 19, 2002
Tegretol 200mg am and bedtime
Risperdal 3 mg bedtime
Ritalin 5mg, 8 am, noon, 3 pm

Tough AM. Hard to get her up and ready for school. Homework went better today. Gave her a snack and 30 min free time after school before starting. Sensed a rage coming after dinner, took her for a walk and put her in the bath early. Seemed to help. Took about 90 minutes to fall asleep tonight.

Oct. 28, 2002
Moved Risperdal and pm Tegretol to dinnertime

Slightly better AM today. Got up & dressed with not as many tears. Went to psychiatrist today—suggested we move up bedtime meds to dinnertime to see if it helps with getting to sleep. Homework was difficult. She had a lot of math. I had to cover up all the problems with blank paper except the one she was working on. Seemed to ease her anxiety a little. Bedtime was OK but didn't fall asleep until almost midnight.

Oct. 29, 2002
Getting up was very difficult today. She cried almost the entire morning and said how tired she was. Homework was also tough, when I pushed her she started to lose control. I sent her to her room for 15 minutes. She put on some music really loud and slammed her door a few times but it seemed to help and she was able to get a little bit done. Bedtime was better tonight. She was asleep by 9:30!!! Yeah!

Example 2:

3/10/03
Started Ritalin: 5 mg after waking and 5 mg @ 3:00
    —dry mouth for first couple of days

    —seems a little "spaced out" and really quiet

    —seeing little or no change other than she seems sedated

5/13/03
Stopped Ritalin

5/20/03
Started Depakote 125mg am and bedtime
    —Using sprinkle caps. Hated with applesauce, tolerates in yogurt and ice
      cream

6/06/03
same meds
    —mood seems to be better after two weeks

    —no noticeable side effects

    —blood test results: Valproic acid level=105

7/15/03
same meds
    —actually played with a friend for two hours without any problems

    —didn't get upset when she lost a game

Example 3:

Date/time/ activity	What happened	Behavior/Duration	How it resolved/ what happened next
Sat. am. At friend's after sleep-over	no more Lucky Charms	threw his bowl across the room and yelled for 20 min. that he wanted to go home	Friend's mom kept refocusing him on the need to get ready so he could see mom sooner. He still yelled about the cereal but got ready while he was yelling.
Sun. aft. at Birthday party	lost a birthday game	screamed at the mom, grabbed the prize from the kid who won	I took him out to the car for 20 min. When he couldn't calm down, I took him home before he could get his party bag and told him he had to have 3 problem-free playdates before going to another birthday party.
Mon. eve.	said VCR not working right	yelled, hit, and pushed the VCR off the shelf	Stopped after Dad reminded him that there wouldn't be any more movies if he broke the VCR.

8

Psychiatric Medications and Kids

Many books are available to help you understand the technical aspects of the medications that are used to treat Bipolar Disorder. This chapter is primarily designed to help you understand what's involved in using these drugs and how to handle the parental responsibilities involved in caring for a child who is taking psychiatric medication. Please consult your doctor for specific information as it relates to your child's particular situation.

Fortunately, research in psychiatric medication is constantly going on. What is now the most current treatment for Bipolar Disorder in children is not what it was five years ago or even one year ago. We are learning more about it every day. Remember again that educating yourself will decrease feelings of fear and lack of control. The more you know, the more confident you'll be in decision making, and the more comfortable you'll be with those decisions.

WHAT YOU NEED TO KNOW

▲ Bipolar Disorder is caused by a chemical imbalance in the brain. The brain uses chemicals to communicate signals about how we think, feel, perceive, and react. Therefore, when the chemicals are out of balance, it affects mood and behavior. Psychiatric medications help to establish a more typical balance of brain chemistry.

▲ Every medication has a generic name that is used by all manufacturers who make it. This is the chemical name that describes the ingredients. The medication name that you will likely hear used more frequently is the brand name. This is the name that the manufacturer gives it and uses to market it. For example, acetaminophen is the generic name for Tylenol, ibuprofen is the generic name for Advil and Motrin, and methylphenidate is the generic name for Ritalin. Some doctors write prescriptions for the generic name, and some write it for the brand name. If you're not sure that the prescription is for the right medication, ask! If your doctor prescribes a specific brand medication, ask the doctor whether or not it's okay to get the generic form. If the doctor prescribes and wants you to use a specific brand, tell the pharmacy not to substitute with the generic. To avoid this problem, remind the doctor to mark "brand only" on the prescription. Don't switch back and forth or substitute generic and brand name medications unless the doctor tells you to. Your child may not have the same response. It is possible that your child may find brand name Ritalin, for example, more effective than the generic methylphenidate or vice versa. Also, if you have insurance that only covers generic medications, make sure to tell the doctor so he/she can manage the medication with that in mind. It's sad that a doctor sometimes has to make decisions based on what an insurance company wants, but it's a reality of today's healthcare system.

▲ The Food and Drug Administration (FDA) approves medications for certain uses. All medications available in the U.S. have received FDA approval for some type of use. Less than 25% of all these medications list uses for children. A lack of FDA approval for use in children does not necessarily reflect lack of safety or effectiveness. What it does reflect is a lack of controlled studies. Because the pediatric market is small and there are ethical issues related to testing in children, formal research into the effects of medications on children is rarely done. Despite this, nearly all drugs currently marketed in the U.S. have been used by children. The medications can be used for children because "common clinical practice" shows that they can work. This means that most of the information about the results in children is based on actual use by individual patients, small studies by individual psychiatrists, and results from adult studies. So, don't be nervous if the medications your doctor prescribes aren't specifically approved for use in children or for your child's specific symptoms. The use of medications for different symptoms than the ones for which they received FDA approval is called prescribing "off label." This means that the manufacturer has published no specific dosage, administration or side effect information specifically for children. However, your doctor will use pediatric dosing guidelines that are published by pediatric experts, modifications of adult dosage guidelines, and documented clinical results from use in children. The FDA recognizes that in certain circumstances, off label uses of approved products are appropriate, rational, and accepted medical practice. Prescribing a medication for an off label indication is common in the treatment of children and is not considered experimental if based on sound scientific evidence.

▲ Many medications that are used for psychiatric purposes are also used for other medical reasons. In fact, the medical reasons, such as epilepsy or pain relief, may be the primary FDA-approved usage. Through general usage, they may have been discovered to help other symptoms. Bottom line: don't worry if you find out that the Tegretol your 6 year-old is using for mood stabilization is also being used by your colleague's epileptic daughter to control seizures or that the Zyban your neighbor is taking to help him stop smoking is actually the same medication as the Wellbutrin your child is taking to help her mood.

▲ Dosages don't necessarily depend on the child's size or age like many over-the-counter medications do. In fact, many times children will actually be on higher dosages than adults because they metabolize, absorb, or eliminate medications from their systems differently. Don't be concerned or surprised if your child is on Zoloft and takes the same dosage as your husband or if you meet another mom and her 185-pound, 18 year-old boy is on a lower dosage of Zyprexa than your 60-pound, 7 year-old girl.

▲ Like any other type of medication, psychiatric medications do have side effects. You will likely find yourself one time or a million times asking yourself if the benefits outweigh these adverse effects. You and your child will need to decide together which side effects are acceptable and which are not. Some examples of side effects might be upset stomach, fatigue, dry mouth, tremors, and weight gain. Many children really struggle with the side effects of medication on top of everything they already have to deal with. Weight gain seems to be a real issue for children especially as they reach the pre-teen and teen-aged years.

▲   Not much is known about the long-term side effects of some of these medications. These are crucial, even painful decisions to make for our children. At times it may feel impossible to fathom putting a child on a medication that may cause future infertility, for example. But you have to look at the whole picture. You have to prioritize the effects and side effects and make the best decision you can at that particular time. Even though it's difficult to accept that a medication might affect some aspect of your child's future health, his current behaviors and moods also have long-term effects. Your child's symptoms stunt social, mental and intellectual development as well as make him (and everyone around him) unhappy. And in some cases, not medicating a Bipolar child might make the Bipolar Disorder more severe, perhaps even resulting in the child hurting himself or someone else before he's even lived long enough to experience any potential long-term side effects from medications. Most parents decide that the short-term benefits outweigh the potential long-term risks. There are things you can do, however, to decrease the risk to some extent. Make sure that your child is regularly receiving the appropriate medical tests to check for side effects. Read about the medications your child takes and make sure your "team" is up to date on the latest research. Adjust your medication choices if and when it becomes necessary. Don't be afraid to subscribe to journals or attend seminars that are given for professionals. The more educated you are, the easier it will be to make decisions.

▲   There are different classes or categories of medications used to treat the symptoms of Bipolar Disorder and the conditions that often occur along with it. These classes include mood stabilizers, stimulants, anti-depressants, anti-anxiety medications, and anti-psychotics. Don't be surprised or concerned if your child needs medications from more than one of these categories. Most children with Bipolar Disorder respond best to a combination rather than just one single medication.

WHAT TO ASK BEFORE STARTING ANY NEW MEDICATION

Ask the doctor the following questions:

▲ What is the name of the medication (brand and generic)?

▲ What type of medication is it? How does it work? (Although for some medications, we don't really know how they work.)

▲ How might this medication react with other medications my child is taking?

▲ What do you expect it to do for my child?

▲ What is its history of effectiveness for children with Bipolar Disorder?

▲ What are the short-term side effects? How long can they last?

▲ What are the possible long-term side effects?

▲ What is the starting dosage of this medication?

▲ What is the usual dosage range?

▲ How is this medication monitored? Will my child need blood tests, EKGs or other types of tests? If so, what exactly will you be monitoring?

▲ What symptoms should I look for that might indicate a negative effect?

▲ Are there any symptoms for which I should contact you immediately?

▲ How long does it usually take to begin to notice the effects of this medication?

▲ Are there any other medications or foods I should have my child avoid while taking this medication?

▲ Do you have any printed material about this medication that I can take home to read?

▲ Are there any contraindications that affect whether my child goes on or stays on this medication?

THE PHARMACIST: YOUR NEW BEST FRIEND

It's not enough just to use a good pharmacy. It's also a good idea to consistently use one pharmacist so he/she can spot dosage issues, identify combinations of medications that are problematic, and be willing to serve as a resource for your medication-related questions. Find out that pharmacist's working schedule and ask for him/her when you arrive so you can develop a personal relationship. The pharmacist will then be aware of your child's situation and be familiar enough with her case to answer your questions, whether related to prescription or over-the-counter medications.

> *"My son was having a very difficult time swallowing his medication. I tried everything I could think of. When I spoke to the pharmacist about it, she was unbelievably helpful. She ended up crushing the medication and making a liquid form with a raspberry flavor. It was a miracle for us. The daily battle and tears were gone. I was so grateful."* (Cynthia)

Prescriptions and the pharmacist:

Just knowing about the medication that your child has been prescribed isn't enough. You also need to make sure that your child actually receives the right medication and that you know how to administer it properly. It's a lot easier to do this while you're still at the store than to call and possibly have to go back.

▲ Read the label to make sure you understand all the instructions.

▲ When asking questions or getting information on medications, make sure you are speaking with the pharmacist—not the pharmacy technician.

▲ Look at the pills. Question the pharmacist if they are a different size, shape or color than you've previously received.

▲ If you don't recognize the name of the medication, ask the pharmacist. It might be a different brand name or the generic version. Don't substitute unless you check with your doctor first.

▲ Check and follow the storage instructions on the label and insert.

▲ Ask the pharmacist before crushing, cutting, or dissolving tablets.

▲ If the prescription doesn't include specific information, warnings, or precautions, ask the pharmacist if there is any additional information you should have.

▲ Ask the pharmacist before giving your child an over-the-counter medication. Some will interact poorly with prescription medications. If you are still not sure, ask your doctor.

▲ Make sure you are clear about how and when to give the medication (on an empty stomach, with a meal or milk, first thing in the morning, etc.).

▲ If your child is having a hard time taking a medication, ask the pharmacist for suggestions. Some medications can be made into an elixir or come in more kid-friendly forms, such as sprinkle caps (capsules that can be opened so the contents can be sprinkled on food) or chewables. You can also try giving a pill in a spoonful of peanut butter, ice cream or yogurt. Your pharmacist will likely have some other good suggestions for you.

▲ If your pharmacist doesn't seem overly helpful or attentive, find a new one! Even if it isn't quite as convenient a location, it will be well worth having a competent, knowledgeable, and kind pharmacist as a member of your "team."

▲ It is critical to remember that as good as your pharmacist may be, people do make mistakes. Mistakes happen at pharmacies all the time. As with all other areas of our healthcare system, professionals are extremely busy. There will be many times when a pharmacy technician will be the one to fill your child's prescription. Check everything before giving it to your child.

♥   *One time after returning from the pharmacy, I went to give Julie her meds. The pill looked pretty much the same. It was the same color and shape, it even had the same writing on the pill, but it seemed a slightly different size than usual. I decided to trust my instincts and I called the pharmacy. It turned out that I had been given the right medication but the wrong dose. The pills they gave me were three times the dosage they were supposed to be! Thank goodness I checked.*

Some other tips to help make giving medication safer and easier include:

▲   Use a medication storage system that gives you compartments so you can sort and store several days worth of pills. This takes longer up front, but makes it much easier to dispense pills during the days that follow as well as reduces the risk of missed doses.

▲   Ask the pharmacist for syringes or cups that are specially designed to measure and dispense liquid medication. Household spoons vary in volume and are not accurate enough to use for medications.

▲   Liquid forms of some medications can be dangerous because the ingredients may not stay mixed together. The amount of active ingredient can vary from the first doses from the top of the bottle to the last doses from the bottom, making some doses too weak while others are too strong. Check with your pharmacist about how to avoid this problem.

▲   Make sure your child is actually swallowing the medication. Children will hide medication in their cheeks and spit it out later. They also may either throw it away and never take it or hoard it to take it all at once.

MANAGING MEDICATIONS

Never expect to be done managing your child's medications. This isn't a disorder that has a standard treatment. Not only are there lots of different medications that might help, but there are many different combinations and dosages that can be changed to create different effects for your child's particular brain chemistry. You can anticipate that managing medications will be an on-going, significant part of your role as a parent of a Bipolar child. The following suggestions can help make it easier.

▲ Keep copious notes in your mood or medication log, you'll be glad you did. Log all the medication doses, changes in behavior and mood, as well as any side effects.

▲ Know the expected side effects. Also know the extreme side effects that warrant immediate action.

▲ Be in close contact with the doctor when your child starts any new medication. Talk to your doctor about the typical initial side effects and their expected duration. Talk about what effects and side effects your child is experiencing. Your child may initially exhibit side effects that may get better or change over time. It may take awhile for your child's body to adjust, but once she's gotten used to the medication, some of the side effects may go away.

"When Perry first started on his antidepressant he was tired, lethargic, and had a queasy stomach. The doctor kept telling me to give it some time. After about three weeks, just when I was about to throw in the towel, the sluggishness got better and the nausea subsided." (Hailey)

▲ Some side effects may be just too much for your child to handle. There are probably other medication choices that address the same symptoms. Talk to your doctor about switching to another drug that might work better for your child's system.

▲ Really listen to your child about what side effects are and aren't acceptable to him. Be willing to change medications if one is causing side effects that feel intolerable to him.

▲ If your child seems overly fatigued or has a hard time getting to sleep at night, talk to the doctor about changing the time of day your child takes her medication or splitting the dose and taking it two times per day.

▲ Your child is constantly growing and changing. If you know she's having a major growth spurt, has a significant weight change, or is showing signs of puberty, it's important to discuss medication and/or dosage changes with your doctor. Medications can even become more or less effective for no apparent reason, and new symptoms that need to be treated will likely occur.

▲ It is common for Bipolar children to need a combination of more than one medication. This process of finding the right combination at the right dosages can be very frustrating, scary, confusing, and take a very long time. Don't get discouraged! It is more than worth the effort to find the combination that works for your child. Keep in mind that your child's brain is different from every other child's brain, so his medication "cocktail" could be different as well. This may not be the "happy hour" that you had in mind, but it can be the difference between your child living a happy, healthy life or not.

▲ If your child is taking four different medications, it doesn't mean that she's twice as ill as a child who only takes two. Oftentimes, it's the combinations that work best, and different combinations work differently in different people.

▲ Don't be alarmed or surprised if medication adjustments are more common than not. Your child's body and brain are growing and constantly changing. Making changes is a necessary part of proper medication management.

▲ If you start to feel panicked or overwhelmed when you are facing a medication change, upping a dose, adding a new medication, tapering off of one that is not working, etc., keep reminding yourself why you're doing this. You're trying to find out what will work best, at that moment in time, for your child's current situation. You're not trying to find the ultimate, final answer. You have not failed or made bad choices if medication changes become appropriate.

▲ If you're ever tempted to just stop all the medications to see what happens, remember that if your child had any other illness, you wouldn't think of withholding any medications that might make him better. In addition, suddenly stopping medications can worsen the course of the disorder and make mood changes more severe, making them harder to treat.

▲ This is going to be an ongoing process, but as your child matures, changes and learns, she may eventually become more able to control some of her moods and behaviors with less medication.

♥ *Medication? Unimaginable and hopeful at the same time. On the one hand, it was a huge relief to think that we may have a solution, and to be honest, one that didn't require hours on end of behavior modification technique implementation and planning. As a matter of fact, after all the psychologist appointments, books and parenting techniques, the idea of doing something as easy and fast as giving Julie a pill was a bit thrilling. On the other hand, I felt so guilty. I still had some of the same preconceived notions about medication and mental illness as many other people. It felt like a life sentence for Julie and for me. Was it right to medicate a child? Would she be "drugged" or be a different person on medication? Did this make me a failure as a parent or was this the new hope I needed for the future? Well, here's where I started working on my unofficial "pediatric psychopharmacology" degree. "Trial" and "error" became my new middle names. One day, shortly after starting on Ritalin, she actually fell asleep on her desk at school. I felt like such a horrible mother and I was sure the school staff thought the same. Just when I was ready to give up, I started to see small changes—a tantrum that I was able to soothe, a morning without crying, a sweet gesture to her brother. And then one day she came home from school with a picture that she had drawn of herself. I had to excuse myself to the restroom when I saw it. In the bathroom I cried and cried, but they were tears of happiness and relief. Julie had drawn the first picture of herself EVER with a smile on her face.*

Julie's first ever picture of herself with a smile on her face!

OTHER PEOPLE'S REACTIONS TO MEDICATING YOUR CHILD

You will make painstaking decisions for your child's well-being. You will educate yourself, make informed choices, and do what you think is the best thing for your child at every turn. It is not easy, but you'll do it. That should be the end of the hard part, but it is not. After all this, you will have people who tell you that you are poisoning your child, that you are turning her into a drug addict, that you are just too lazy to parent her properly so you take the easy way out, or that you are a brainwashed victim of the money hungry drug companies . . . did we forget anything? You'll probably feel at times as if you have to keep it a secret for fear of being judged and having your child be judged. You will see celebrities who are crusading against medicating children, news stories talking about the Columbine killer who was on medication that made him psychotic, and email jokes circulating calling Ritalin "the babysitter of the 21st century." Yet again, you will face it, confront it, rise above it, and do what is best for your child. This is your job, this is your responsibility to your child . . . but that doesn't make it easy to do.

> ♥ *It's gotten much easier over time, but I have felt so judged by other people because of Julie's medications. It's funny, because it is not only by uneducated or inexperienced people, I almost expect it from them, but even doctors, therapists, nurses and pharmacists at times have not hidden their surprise and dismay. I hate it when I have to take her to a new dentist or fill out school forms. I inevitably get to the portion of the form that asks you to list any medications your child is taking. It seems so easy for people to make sweeping generalizations about you and your child based just on this information. One time at the pediatrician's office we saw the nurse practitioner because it was a Saturday. She was prescribing antibiotics for an infected toe and casually asked if Julie was taking any other medications. I gave her the "list" and waited for that disapproving glance. She actually looked at me very kindly and said, "You must be doing a wonderful job, I never would have known. She seems to be doing so well." I was so touched that I actually wrote her a letter a few days later. She had no idea how wonderful it was to be supported and acknowledged instead of judged.*

"It's funny to watch people's faces when Joey casually mentions that he takes medicine to help him stop worrying so much. I'm so thrilled that he's comfortable talking about it that I don't care what they think. I did get a bit upset, though, when a woman told him that worrying is useless. Obviously, if he is taking medication, he can't just stop worrying based on her advice!" (Sheryl)

♥   *Sheryl opened one of my kitchen cabinets one day to get a glass. She was shocked to see that it was full of prescription medications. Even though she knows everything there is to know about my kids, their treatment, and my life, it clearly disturbed her to see a row after row of prescription bottles like that.*

"It drives me crazy when people who have had plastic surgery, wear glasses, and dye their hair have a hard time understanding why my child takes psychiatric medication. As far as I'm concerned, anything that helps a person feel, behave or function better emotionally or physically is a good thing." (Fran)

SECTION FOUR:

Having a Bipolar Child in the Family

9

The Realities of Your Daily Life

Regardless of whether you just got the diagnosis or you've known for awhile, you're certainly aware that your parenting experience is very different from that of a parent whose child is neurotypical. Having a Bipolar child affects every aspect of your life as well as your child's. You'll be dealing with medication, doctors, schoolteachers and friends. You'll be trying to parent your other children as well as your Bipolar child. You'll be juggling what your Bipolar child needs from you with what you need for yourself and everyone else in the family.

Since your child has a disease that causes behavioral symptoms, you will be thinking about your child's behavior almost constantly, when she's doing well and when she's not. The tendency for your child's behavior to "spiral" out of control with little or no provocation, along with the need for you to help her get back into control as soon as possible, will be a major focus of your parenting experience and daily responsibilities.

As we've said before, having a diagnosis and the support of medical professionals isn't going to suddenly make things better. But, on the positive side, you can start to attribute a lot of your child's negative behaviors to the chemical processes in her brain. It will feel good to stop worrying that you're doing something wrong and start learning about how to implement techniques that have helped other Bipolar kids.

Hopefully, you will also gain the wisdom to know when there is nothing you can do.

On the flip side, while your friends are driving to soccer practice, birthday parties and dance lessons, you'll be driving to psychiatrist and therapy appointments, the pharmacy and blood tests. Your child's Bipolar Disorder will continue to be a major focus of your life. If you just got the diagnosis, finding good therapists and constantly monitoring your child for effects and side effects of medication may feel like all you have time to do. Even when you've been dealing with it for a while, there will always be a part of you that's watching and waiting for your child to have a difficult episode.

> ♥ *My life with Julie? How can something so complex be described? Julie is an incredible, wonderful, intense, exhausting, all-consuming child. She is a "force" as my mother describes her. She is a tiny child (negative 5th percentile for height and weight), yet she takes up an enormous amount of space. She can make you laugh, cry, and seethe all within a span of a few minutes. She has been atypical in many ways from the moment she was born.*

> *"There were never many breaks from Katie. Baby-sitters hardly ever came twice and it seemed a lot to ask from family and friends because she was so demanding. I left her with a neighbor once for around 2 hours. When I returned, she was holding Katie, Katie was crying, and had been crying the entire time I was gone. I never get any time away from her."* (Katherine)

A DAY IN THE LIFE OF THE PARENT OF A BIPOLAR CHILD

Following is a list of some of the activities that you have to do in addition to running a home, working, "typical" parenting, and having a personal life. If anyone wonders why you're so busy and tired, share this list with him or her.

▲ Dispensing medication

▲ Going to doctors' appointments

▲ Going to the pharmacy

▲ Expending tremendous amounts of energy trying to get your child to accomplish basic tasks of daily life, such as brushing teeth and getting dressed

▲ Meeting with or talking to school teachers and counselors

▲ Observing your child's behavior and helping her avoid spiraling

▲ Maintaining a mood log

▲ Maintaining a medication log

▲ Supervising your child when she's with siblings

▲ Supervising your child when she's with friends

▲ Taking your child to get blood tests

▲ Submitting claims to the insurance company

▲ Dealing with the insurance company

▲ Doing the daily chores that a typical child would handle independently, such as cleaning his room and making his bed

▲ Deciding how to appropriately respond to misbehavior in order to provide a learning lesson and to avoid a rage

▲ Going to therapy appointments for yourself to help you handle stress and keep perspective

▲ Getting up in the middle of the night to check on your child or be with her if she's awake

▲ Rearranging your schedule to take your child's mood into consideration (e.g. rescheduling a haircut or play date if she's raging at the time you're supposed to go)

▲ Implementing behavior modification techniques, such as reward charts or point systems

▲ Reading parenting books

▲ Researching Bipolar Disorder

▲ Watching for effects and side effects of medication

▲ Worrying about your child, your effectiveness as a parent, the decisions that you're making, the effects of the medications on your child's body, etc.

▲ Hoping and fearing for the future

> ♥ *Sometimes I think I should introduce myself as "Cindy—I have a Bipolar child—Singer."*

You have to accept that there will be ups, downs, and constant change in your daily life and that your experiences will be different from other parents'. This is what your "normal" is. Like Bipolar Disorder, your role as a parent will have extremes. You are already familiar with the difficult, painful feelings that you experience. There will be many times when your moods mirror your child's. But, remember that parents of typical children may never experience the intense, gut-wrenching joy you'll have when your child gets off to school without having had a battle, does well on a school project you thought was going to be a nightmare, or has a really successful play date. One could say there is a certain amount of bipolarity in our emotions, just as there is in our children's behaviors.

Even when you think you have your child all figured out, new symptoms will pop up. Think of it as a tunnel: although it's slowly being built, no traffic can get through until it is completely open. In our children's brains, new pathways are constantly being developed, but until the connections are complete, the symptoms may not appear. There's no way to control or predict when they will. The only constant, as the saying goes, is change.

> ♥ *Julie definitely brings out the best and worst in me as a mother and as a person. I have learned to be as tough as a drill sergeant, as patient as a saint, and as loving as a mother—even when she is anything but lovable. This is definitely not what I expected. If you had told me 12 years ago what my life would be like with a child, I never would have believed you. If you told me I would be physically restraining my child on a regular basis, that I would give my daughter anti-psychotic medication at the age of 6, that I would spend*

more time in doctors' offices and laboratories than on the sidelines of a soccer field, or that there would be days that I wasn't sure if I was capable of caring for my own child, I would've called you a liar. But, this is my life and this is my beloved child. I cannot tell you how many times I have sat in my car on the driveway dreading going inside my own home, not knowing if I can face one more rage, one more scream, or one more hurtful word. But I make my way back in every time.

PARENTING STRATEGIES TO HELP YOUR CHILD

Behavior that is out of control is a primary characteristic of Bipolar Disorder, so managing our children's behaviors is a large part of how we spend our days (and nights). You've probably read enough parenting books to fill the shelves of a small bookstore and found that some of the techniques worked, some didn't, some worked for a while, some didn't work at first but worked later, and everything in between. Following are still more parenting ideas, but they're specifically designed to help you help your Bipolar child who is struggling with out-of-control behavior. Talk with your child's therapist about developing and using a behavior plan, which will give you a specific method for using these and other parenting strategies to change your child's negative behaviors.

Keep in mind that the goal isn't to teach your child how to eliminate all the negative thoughts and behaviors. That's probably impossible. What you're trying to do is to help identify when a problem is about to begin or is just beginning, then to prevent that thought or behavior from "spiraling"—getting worse and worse until it's totally out of control and he's raging.

Look for and document early signs of out of control behavior.

The more familiar you become with your child's patterns, the earlier you will be able to intervene, increasing the possibility of redirecting the behavior. Early signs could be increased activity level, uninhibited behavior, excessive crying, inability to cope with frustration, etc.

"After reading over the last few months of entries in Dori's mood log, I realized that she almost always starts raging just before a transition when she's involved in something that requires concentration, like if she's reading

and we need to leave the house or I call her to dinner when she is doing her homework." (Alicia)

Redirect your child's activity when you begin to see signs of negative behavior.

Examples may be a bath, some type of physical activity, music, a movie, drawing or painting.

> *"When I see Monique pacing around, talking fast and about to lose control, I put out some art supplies, turn on her favorite music, or put on one of her favorite videos. She usually notices and, if the activity has any chance at all of stopping her from raging, she'll start on it herself."* (Marian)

Whenever possible, let your child retain some control over the situation.

Bipolar children hate to feel submissive. Whenever possible give your child two (or more, depending on the age) acceptable choices instead of direct commands. Be very specific and avoid open ended questions or questions that are easy to answer with a "No," such as, "Are you ready to start your homework?" Also avoid giving commands, such as, "It's time to do your homework." Instead, you could say, "Would you like to start your homework in 5 minutes or 10 minutes?" Create goals for your child to make it exciting and competitive to get things done. For example, say, "How fast do you think you can clean your room?" or "Pick ten things to put away." This helps your child feel like she has accomplished something important and helps her predict and identify when she has successfully finished something.

> *"Ryan can't stand being told what to do. That means that many times when I need him to do something I try to think of a strategy to get him to think he chose it on his own. It takes a lot of advance thinking, but it's better than having him lose control or having a fight that could have been fairly easily avoided."* (Margaret)

Use relaxation techniques.

Try yoga, deep breathing, meditation, and listening to soothing music with your child. These are great skills for getting to sleep as well. Some kids like whale, rainfall, or ocean sounds CDs and relaxation/meditation tapes.

> *"Some days, Amber will do yoga with a videotape. It seems to help her calm both her body and her mind. Even when she's not actually doing it, the words and music seem to relax her a bit anyway."* (Allyson)

Get your child moving.

The latest research is showing that exercise actually releases some of the same chemicals in the brain as some of the medications we are giving our children. So, in addition to all the benefits of exercise that we already know, we now know that we can actually change our brain chemistry with even a 10 minute bout of activity.

> *"Instead of sending Matt to time-out, I now have him take the dog for a walk around the block. It's great for the dog, it's much easier on his room, and, more often than not, he returns in a better frame of mind."* (Molly)

Focus relentlessly on positive behavior.

We spend so much time disciplining our children, and some days are definitely worse than others. Look for, praise, and reward positive behavior as much as possible even if it is preceded by and/or followed with bad behavior. It is not only good for your child to be recognized for the good things he does, but it is very beneficial for parents of children with behavior problems to force themselves to focus on the good things that have happened each day.

> *"My refrigerator is covered with reward charts, notes that I post so the whole family knows when Carlo did something positive, and pictures that Carlo drew for me."* (Antonia)

> *"At the end of the day, as a family, we sit down together and each person shares something they are thankful for about each person in the family. It took awhile for us to get the hang of it, but it really feels good to know that everyone is trying to focus on appreciating each other."* (Chloe)

You may already have tried many different types of reward systems to motivate your child to show positive behavior. Some may have worked for a while; others may not have worked at all. If you take some of the standard reward ideas and modify them to better suit a Bipolar child, you might find one that works for your child. The trick is to make sure you select behaviors appropriate for your child. Other children might be expected to make their beds, straighten their room, and get their backpacks ready as one "morning chores" expected behavior of the day. The morning behaviors for your Bipolar child may be "get out of bed" and "get dressed" as two separate behaviors. Your child's expected behaviors will also include not doing negative behaviors, such as "don't hit your brother," as well as doing positive behaviors.

It's also important that the expected behaviors and the rewards be age-appropriate so they are interesting and realistic enough for your child. For example, it might be unrealistic to think that your child can say nice things all day. Maybe you should start with giving your child a star, sticker or point every time she says something nice. Then, after she's improved her ability to communicate nicely, expect her to say only nice things for an hour, a whole morning, or an afternoon. If she gets good at that, make it all day. As you're making changes to the expected behaviors, adjust the rewards as well. At the beginning you might let her choose a treat to eat after earning four stars in a day. Later, she might earn a treat after more stars. Remember to always have "freebies" which are behaviors your child has mastered that she can be rewarded for. Add only one difficult new behavior at a time. Start with a foundation of easier tasks and build on it slowly.

Think carefully about what you want to use for rewards. It's unrealistic and inappropriate to think that you can take your child somewhere special every day as a reward. Also make sure you don't give too many food-related rewards. The best rewards are about increased privileges and attention, not tangible gifts or expensive activities. Make the difficult, expensive and time-consuming rewards, such as going to the movies, renting a movie, or going out for ice cream, really special. They should be hard to earn but achievable goals. Some ideas for rewards that are easy to offer, but important to most children include: not having to make the bed, getting an extra story at bedtime, getting to stay up 15 minutes later, watching an extra 30 minutes of TV, choosing a sticker or very small toy, and getting to choose what's for dinner.

♥ *One of Julie's favorite rewards was to be "the boss of mommy" for 15 minutes.*

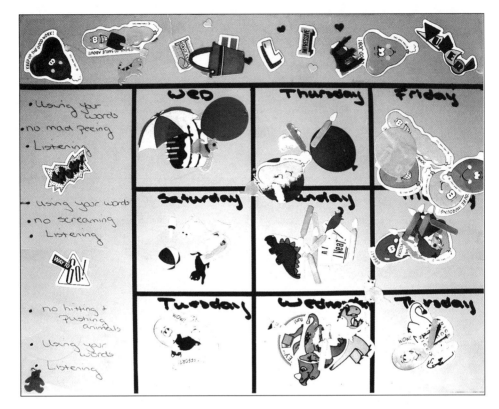

These are two reward charts that worked for Julie.
The first was used when she was 5. The second was used when she was 9.

Teach your child how to be aware of, quantify, and identify her feelings and emotions.

Teach words for describing feelings. One option is to use colors to describe feelings—green for happy, red for angry, blue for sad, yellow for frustrated, etc. Have your child put different colored pipe cleaners, beads, or buttons in a clear jar to show how he is feeling if it is too difficult for him to discuss. Have your child rate his feelings. "On a scale of 1-10, how angry are you right now?" Draw a picture of a glass and have your child show you how much of a certain emotion he is feeling by coloring in how full the glass would be. Or, you could have him fill a real glass to the appropriate level. For younger children, use "green light," "yellow light," and "red light" or a "thermometer" to describe the intensity of feelings like anxiety, silliness or anger. Draw several faces with different emotions.

BEHAVIORS

Behavior	Points
Get up nicely	5
Brush teeth	3
Get dressed nicely	3
Say something nice	5
Do something nice for someone	5
Follow directions the 1st time	5
Do homework	10
Read for 15 minutes	7
Go to bed without a fight	10

MENU

Item	Points
Dessert	10
30 minutes of TV	10
Pick from the treat jar	15
Have a friend over to play	20
30 min special time w/ Dad	20
Stay up 15 minutes late	30
Trip to DQ	50
Go to a movie	75
New CD	100
Sleepover	100

Let your child pick the one that describes how she is feeling. Have your child draw a picture of himself to describe his feelings or draw a pie chart to show how much of the time he's feeling happy, sad, mad, scared, and worried.

"Joey's psychiatrist asked him to draw a pie chart to show how much he was experiencing different emotions. I was shocked to see how little he felt

'happy.' He also created a big section where he put all the emotions together. After discussing how he felt when all the emotions were happening together, he and the psychiatrist decided that this section could also be considered to be a 'worry' section. As his Serzone started to take effect, Joey would tell me that the 'happy part' was getting bigger and the worried part was getting smaller. The pie chart is a great tool to help him communicate about how he's feeling." (Sheryl)

Joey's pie charts.

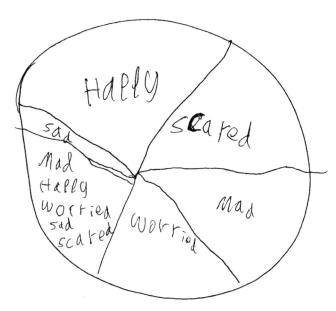

Involve your child in recognizing her own early signs of out of control behavior.

Say, "You look really angry." Or, "You look like you are getting very frustrated. Are you feeling like you are going to lose control?" It might take your child years to learn to recognize or predict her own behavior, but keep trying to help her learn these skills, even if it seems fruitless right now. It would be a wonderful gift for your child to possess, if not now, maybe as an adult.

> *"Yesterday, Madeline asked me if it looked like she was getting her angry face. I was thrilled that she was expressing that she felt like she was getting angry before it became obvious to everyone. I told her that it did look like she was a bit grumpy and praised her up and down for noticing it before she was out of control. I was so excited I let her decide where to go out to dinner."* (Michele)

Have someone else help you.

There may be times when you need to step out of the equation. This is a good strategy when it seems your child just wants to pick a fight with you or is trying to push every last one of your buttons. Let other people help! It can be hard to do this, even with your spouse, but the more you do it, the easier it will become.

> *"The last time our son lost control and was practically beating up my wife, I told her to call a friend and go out to lunch while I handled the situation. I can't believe how grateful she was, even though she did protest that she couldn't possible leave him in that condition. After she returned and realized that both Michael and I had not only survived, but also calmed down, she was very relieved. It actually was great for my confidence in handling Michael and I felt really connected to him afterward."* (James)

> *"My schedule is full with driving Lexi to therapy and doctor appointments, going to the pharmacy, meeting with the school, and taking my other children to all their activities. I was so grateful when my mother offered to help with some of the driving. When she drives Lexi to some of the therapy appointments that I don't need to be at, I have time to stay and watch Jayson at his soccer practice or Megan at her softball game. Sometimes Mom drives*

the other kids to their activities and stays and watches. It is such a relief. My Mom gets some grandma time at the same time she is helping me out. I get to spend important, uninterrupted time with each of my kids." (Leesa)

Be prepared to leave any social situation that your child cannot handle.

If you know up front, before going into any situation, that you might have to leave, it can help you feel more relaxed and in control. Have a signal with your partner to indicate that you need to leave. Agree ahead of time that if either parent gives the signal, quick goodbyes will be said and you will leave right away. You may want to have another signal, too, to indicate that your child is not doing well and you need to leave soon.

"My husband just needs to look at me to know when I think we need to leave because Brittany is about to lose it. He says he always knows from a certain way that I purse my mouth. He also knows that there is no debating the decision once that look appears on my face!" (Deanna)

"The first few times that I told Robin we would leave if she didn't behave appropriately, she didn't believe me. Things got even worse when I dragged her away from the playground or out of the movie theater. Now she knows I'm serious. All I have to do is start to count to five on my fingers for her to know that she'd better get in control. It doesn't always work, but it makes it easier to explain why we're leaving if I get all the way up to five." (Lilly)

After a bad episode, talk to your child about it.

After the rage is over, talk about what does and doesn't work. Be very specific. "Does it help when I hug you?" "Does it help when I tell you I love you?" "When you are so angry, what can I do to help you feel better?" "Do you like to be left alone when you feel angry or frustrated?" "What should I do the next time you are feeling that way?"

"I wrote Sophie a note telling her what I think she did well the last time she had a difficult day and asking what I could have done to help her more. She gave me a picture showing me saying 'I love you' while she was kicking the door. That picture said a thousand words." (Jean)

Teach your child about accountability, apologizing, forgiveness, and repairing relationships.

Our children must learn that even though they cannot always control their behaviors, they are still responsible for them. There are always consequences to all our actions whether they are in our control or not. If your child broke something in a rage of anger, he is responsible for fixing or replacing it. If he hurt someone's feelings, he needs to apologize. Relationships will undoubtedly be injured when emotions run so high. There will need to be mending. Teach this by example as well. There will likely be many times you feel like you could have handled a situation with your child differently. Tell him this and say you are sorry if you lost your temper or said something hurtful as well.

"The last time Evan broke something on purpose, I didn't get mad, I just took the cost of replacing it out of his allowance the next week. He didn't like it, but he understood it." (Ken)

"Cody just couldn't apologize to his friend after calling him horrible names and literally kicking him out the door when they had an argument. I convinced him that he should email an apology. That way, I could help him say the appropriate things and avoid having them argue with each other again." (Ashley)

Teach your child self-soothing skills.

Talk to your child during a calm time about things she can do herself when she is angry, sad, or out of control. Make a list together and have it handy for your child to look at when she needs to.

"Isabella keeps a stack of calm music CD's, a special brush for rubbing her skin, and several scented lotions by her bed. We call them her Calm Things. She also has a beanbag chair in her room that seems to be a place where she can try to relax." (Sue)

Work on gaining the wisdom to recognize when there's nothing you can do and know that this is NOT a failure.

Even if you try all these techniques and make up some of your own, there will still be times that your child's spiraling behavior needs to just run its course. It can seem as if there is this enormous amount of energy that needs to be released from our children's bodies. There just isn't anything you can do about that other than make sure not to think you did something wrong and try to learn from the situation. It can be the best thing for your child just to be left alone and, sometimes, it's what we need to do for ourselves as well.

"I was really proud of myself last night. Christina was so angry and violent that I just knew she was just going to have to tire herself out before she'd stop. I didn't fuel the fire by arguing with her, attempting to soothe her, or even getting personally involved in it. I actually think she calmed down faster without me getting involved than she would have if I had tried to make things better." (Trina)

10
Managing Bipolar Disorder's Effects on The Whole Family

Having a Bipolar child in the family is physically, emotionally, and spiritually all-encompassing. It tugs at the seams of all family relationships—parent, child, sibling, and spouse. Bipolar is a mood disorder, but it affects almost every aspect of a child's life. In turn, it affects almost all aspects of a parent's life, even becoming the parent's life. It tries to take over, and creating balance is extremely important but also incredibly difficult. This chapter will help you find a balance between taking care of the rest of your family and caring for your Bipolar child. (We will talk more about balancing your responsibilities and taking care of yourself in Chapter 11.)

Our other children and our partner need us, and we need them even when it feels like we don't have one more ounce to give. There's no doubt that they, too, are dramatically affected, and we need to create some sense of a normal life for them as well as for ourselves. It's not enough to only focus on helping your Bipolar child be okay. The whole family has to be okay. You cannot focus only on external situations such as school and social activities. You also have to work on life at home.

BALANCING THE NEEDS OF ALL YOUR CHILDREN

Every parent of more than one child feels like they're almost constantly juggling the needs of each of their children, even if the children don't have special needs. For you, like every other parent, the most important thing is to deal with each child based on his or her specific needs and personality. The reality is that your Bipolar child will take a lot of attention. Your other children may not have such urgent and immediate needs for attention. So, if you can't give each child the same amount of attention, you have to find other ways to purposefully show your other children that their feelings and needs are as important as those of your Bipolar child. In a household that often revolves around the moods of a Bipolar child, this can be tricky, but it's healthy for you, for your other children, and even for your Bipolar child, who does need to learn that the world doesn't always revolve around him.

Try to come up with special times to be with your other child(ren) when your Bipolar child is occupied with another parent or friend. Allow your other child(ren) to do special activities with friends. Find ways to do something that is especially meaningful even if it doesn't take up a lot of time. For example, make your other child's favorite meal, buy a surprise gift that she had really been wanting, or write her a note that tells her how much you love her, how wonderful she is, and how much you treasure her.

> *"Kyle can't stand it when I pay attention to his sister. He will try anything to get my attention away from her. Sometimes I even risk putting him into a rage by saying that I can't help him right now because I'm helping Melanie. I don't want either of them to think that Kyle's needs always come first. In fact, sometimes when he's raging, and I know that nothing I do will make any difference, I make a conscious effort to focus my attention on Melanie. She needs to know that her feelings are important during Kyle's rages too."*
> (Linda)

Even if you do take steps to do special things for your other child(ren), though, there will still be times that they resent not having your attention. If you are only paying attention to your Bipolar child's positive and negative behaviors, your other children will probably start acting out to get some of your attention, too. A key trick is to be aware of how your words and actions toward your Bipolar child affect your other children, not just your Bipolar child. What you say about behavior is important for all of your children regardless of which child is misbehaving. They all need to hear you pointing out what is and isn't acceptable behavior, saying loving things even when they aren't acting lovable, and praising positive behaviors. If you let your Bipolar child get away with poor behavior without saying anything, but discipline your other children for the same types of behaviors without explaining why, they will feel that you are being extremely unfair.

No one in the family has an excuse for not trying to behave well.It's important for your Bipolar child to understand that while he can't control all his feelings and behaviors, he does have to try to behave as well as possible. Your other children need to understand that they have to try to be in control of their behaviors, too. Just as you get involved in different activities for different children based on their unique interests, and discipline them in different ways according what does and doesn't work for each of them, you might need have different expectations of what is acceptable behavior from each of your children. What is acceptable from your Bipolar child may not be acceptable from your non-Bipolar child(ren).

As long as you are consistent in your expectations of each individual child, explain that you treat them each differently because of their unique needs, and that you love them all equally, your children will probably all adjust. That doesn't mean that your neurotypical children won't try to get away with rages, threats or intense anger, but they will learn to understand how to live up to their own potential, respond to different people according to their specific needs and personalities, and control their own behaviors to the best of their abilities. These are important life skills for everyone in the family.

"Hannah actually admitted to me today that she's been acting bad on purpose. She said she wants to get just as much attention as her Bipolar brother gets. She even said that she wants to have Bipolar Disorder, too!" (Leeann)

When you're trying to understand and respond to the symptoms of Bipolar Disorder, it can be hard to keep track of normal, appropriate mental and intellectual development. It's important that you keep up on non-Bipolar aspects of childhood development, both for your Bipolar child and your neurotypical child(ren). Also, try not to keep looking for symptoms of mental illness in your other children. It's certainly something you'll want to be alert for, but your whole experience of parenting shouldn't revolve around watching for mental illness and its symptoms.

Another common worry for parents of more than one child is having to protect your other child(ren)'s physical well-being, not just their emotional well-being. Unfortunately, this isn't a baseless worry. Bipolar children are just as likely to hurt their siblings as their parents and themselves. You do have to make sure not to leave your Bipolar child unattended with a very young child until you are sure that he isn't going to act out against his sibling. You don't want to allow your Bipolar child to rage in a violent way around his siblings. Since it's sometimes hard to control a raging Bipolar child, you might have to remove your other child(ren) from the situation in order to protect them.

> ♥ *One evening I was home alone with Julie and Sam. Julie started raging. She was screaming, throwing and hitting things, and saying that she hated me. I looked across the family room at my 4 year-old son. He had this look on his face. He was scared and confused. Suddenly, I realized that he needed me as much as she needed me at that moment. I realized I actually had to choose which of my children to protect and nurture at that moment. How does a person make a choice like that? I ended up taking Sam out in the cul-de-sac to play hockey. I stood far enough away from him so he couldn't see me crying as I listened to Julie in the house screaming. It was the first time I realized that part of my job was going to be protecting one of my children from the other.*

HAVING MORE THAN ONE SPECIAL NEEDS CHILD

The delicate balancing act of responding to each child's unique needs is even more difficult when you have more than one special needs child. Since you already have one child with a biologically-based and hereditary psychodevelopmental disorder, you have an increased chance of having more than one child with difficulties. Having two children with special needs can feel like having quintuplets. There's nothing different we can suggest to help you cope. Just know that you're not alone, that your challenges truly are much more complex, and that you just have to do what has to be done.

♥   *After waiting for a really long time to get pregnant again, I was thrilled to have Sam, a quiet, cuddly, sweet baby. He rarely fussed. He could sit quietly in his car seat for hours. He didn't seem to care when Julie was raging. I thanked God that I had what I thought must be a "normal" child. When Sam was almost three, his preschool teachers came to me and said that they thought he had a sensory integration problem. He wasn't interacting with his peers and hadn't developed social skills or imaginative play. He would get extremely focused on certain activities and was very set in his ways. He developed very specific, ritualistic ways of doing things and liked everything to always be the same. He watched the same video over and over and over and was really interested in numbers. My friends started to comment on how incredibly quiet Sam was. They would try and try to get him to respond to them, but he just wouldn't interact. I knew he could talk because he could recite all the words to many episodes of his favorite television show. I just thought maybe he wasn't terribly social and maybe he had developed some very strong defense mechanisms to deal with the intensity of our home life.*

At three, Sam could name all the letters and count forward and backward to 80. I knew he was smart, but I was getting more and more feedback about how he wasn't exactly "normal." His social and verbal skills were definitely behind. I just didn't have any sense of how a normal child developed and acted. I knew he wasn't as developmentally advanced as Julie had been, but she was extremely precocious. I was so happy that he wasn't a difficult child that it hadn't seemed important that Sam wasn't terribly verbal or interactive.

After weeks of worry and a very intense fear of opening a whole new can of worms, I took him to be evaluated by the same psychologist who had evaluated Julie. She sent us to a specialist and the diagnosis came back almost immediately. Sam had Asperger's Syndrome, a disorder that is on the autistic spectrum. Suddenly, I was back to square one with adjusting to a devastating diagnosis, educating myself on a syndrome I had never even heard of, finding the appropriate specialists to treat my child, learning parenting skills to meet his unique needs, and coping with everyone else's reactions. I had to implement a rigorous schedule of training sessions to teach Sam language and social interaction skills. I had to give my young child psychiatric medication. I had to adjust my hopes and dreams for my child's future. I had to constantly weigh each child's short and long-term needs. I felt like I was making life-changing decisions all day long. I could not believe this was happening to me again. I began to think that it must be me. I must surely be a terrible parent. How could things go wrong twice?

It took me awhile to adjust to my new schedule. All of a sudden my "easy one" needed me just as much as Julie did. I tried to do as much of his behavioral therapy program as possible when Julie was in school because she would get so jealous. Sometimes it seemed that no matter how hard I tried, one child was going to get less attention and less help than was needed.

Even though it was hard to admit, I needed help. I hired someone to help tutor Sam. I went to my own therapist more often. I found and moved to a neighborhood that had better schools and opportunities for my kids. I got involved in support groups for parents of Bipolar kids. I created a support group for parents of kids with Asperger's Syndrome. My husband got a vasectomy (two kids was definitely enough!), and I coped as best I could. It wasn't necessarily ideal at all times, but it was the best I could do in the situation I was faced with.

DEALING WITH EXTENDED FAMILY

You'd like to think that your extended family members would be the ones most likely to provide you, your family and your Bipolar child with unconditional love and support. While there are likely to be some family members who do, there will probably also be those that don't. Their attitudes may be harder to take than those of skeptical or judgmental friends, neighbors, teachers and doctors. After all, they know you. They should be aware of how hard you're trying to be a good parent and should be able to accept that your child is difficult, even if they don't know about the Bipolar diagnosis. If they do know, they should be willing to accept it and be anxious to learn about it and how it affects your child. They should, but some people just can't find it in themselves to do this, even for a relative.

♥ *We were at a holiday party last year at a cousin's house. There were probably forty people, all extended family. Most of them were relatives that we only see about twice a year. Julie was in one of her hypersensitive moods where everything seems to hurt her feelings and she feels like nothing goes her way. Something very small happened, like one of the other kids didn't want to play what she wanted to play, and Julie got upset and wanted to leave. Before I knew it, I couldn't find her anywhere. I searched for her quietly for a while but after about 15 minutes I began to really panic. Soon after that, everyone at the party was searching for her. We looked all over the house, outside, and even began to search the neighborhood. It seemed like hours, but was probably about a half hour before we found her in the living room behind the couch. She was hiding and listening the entire time. She heard us all looking for her, and she even heard as I started to panic. I wonder how long she would have stayed back there if someone hadn't found her. Needless to say, I was incredibly embarrassed. None of them really know about Julie's problems, but I'm sure there was some talk after that day. I felt so depressed on the way home. I couldn't even go to a family party without something happening that sets us apart from everyone else.*

"When my cousin and I had little girls within three months of each other, we were ecstatic—built in best friends, we hoped! As our children grew and played together, there started to be problems. Jessica was always telling on Monica. My cousin and I talked a lot about parenting techniques and discipline strategies, but nothing worked with Monica. My cousin kept bringing Jessica over, though. Once we got a diagnosis and started treating her Bipolar Disorder, Monica got a lot better. My cousin was the first person I told when I finally admitted to myself that things might actually be getting better for real. I expected her to be thrilled that we had figured out the problem. I was devastated when she told me that she just 'didn't want to expose her daughter to such a serious problem.' What, does she think, it's contagious? What's so different now that we have a diagnosis? I am so hurt. It's just one more hurt on top of everything else and I just don't have the energy to work on this relationship right now. It's her loss. I just wish Jessica had a better role model so she could learn to accept people who are different." (Paula)

"Sometimes I feel a secret pleasure when my relatives' children misbehave. They are always so judgmental when Aaron acts up!" (Kristen)

If the difficult person wasn't related, you'd probably just avoid them in the future. You can't necessarily do that when the problem person is a relative. You may have to make some difficult choices. What would the effects be on your immediate family if you just didn't see a certain relative any more? How would that affect your relationships with the rest of your extended family?

It comes down to weighing each situation. At some point, it may become obvious that a particular relative shouldn't be around your child, so you'll just have to do what it takes to make that happen. In other situations, you may just have to plan carefully to create the best scenario for them to be together, such as making sure that there are lots of kids together, not just your child and the difficult relative's child.

> *"I will go only go to family get-togethers if the kids are going to be running around and playing and there are lots of activities to do. Mason just doesn't do well at formal, sit-down events. At first I resented missing events because of Mason, so we just went and did the best we could. It finally got to the point that it was more trouble than it was worth. If my family would help me out and make me feel like it was okay that Mason wasn't behaving well like all the other kids, I could tolerate it, but dealing with him and their glares the whole time ruined the fun. It's not worth going anymore."* (Blaire)

Unfortunately, even those relatives who are close and understanding may occasionally have difficulty being as supportive and accepting as we would like. As we ourselves know, Bipolar Disorder is a very hard diagnosis to deal with. If we have trouble, it's to be expected that our relatives will to. After all, they had hopes and dreams for our families, too.

> *"My mom has always been incredibly supportive of my struggles with Courtney. But when I first got the diagnosis of Bipolar Disorder, she seemed to withdraw. My feelings got really hurt. I didn't think that my own mother had a problem accepting her grandchild for what she is, but I just couldn't think of any other reason for her to pull away. After a couple of months I asked her what was going on. She told me that she was having an incredibly hard time worrying about what a difficult time her child—me—was having. She just couldn't bear seeing everything I was going through. She felt that she was actually making things worse for me by being around me when she was so upset. Once we talked and shared our feelings, things got a lot better."* (Veronica)

"My extended family is full of people who've been involved in sexual abuse, alcohol abuse, suicide, multiple divorces, teenage pregnancies, gambling problems, school drop-outs, and just generally bad life choices. Many of them very well may have untreated mental illness, too. They are so vocal about their lives and are such bad role models for my daughter that I have made the very difficult decision just not to be around them. I feel like our lives are challenging enough. I hope one day Lily understands my decision. I just have to do what is best for her right now." (Maggie)

YOUR FAMILY'S SOCIAL LIFE

As much as you might like to at times, you and your immediate family can't just exist on your own. Even if your Bipolar child has difficulties with social relationships, the rest of you deserve to have and be with your friends. You'll find out who your true friends are, though, when you have a Bipolar child. As with relatives, some people just can't cope with a difficult situation. Some people just don't know how to be unconditionally supportive. So, here's another example of when you're going to have to make difficult choices about balancing your need to take care of your Bipolar child with the need to take care of yourself and the rest of your family. You're going to have to constantly weigh the pros and cons of having certain people in your lives.

"We have no social life and very few friends. Friends who don't have kids have no tolerance and don't want David around. Friends who do have kids don't want David around their kids. Sometimes I feel like he has leprosy instead of Bipolar Disorder." (Dianna)

"We have become very good friends with a family we met through a Bipolar support group. We all face the same issues, our kids like the same types of activities, and we each discipline, love, support and nurture all of our kids. It feels great to have friends like this." (Kendall)

♥   *Our last neighborhood, from the outside, seemed like a wonderful place to live and raise children. A dream house at the end of a cul-de-sac in upper middle class suburbia with loads of children in the surrounding houses. The first year everything seemed great. We had block parties, play dates, and mom's nights out. Up to this point, Julie was still functioning quite well at* school and outside of the home. As I became closer to the woman who lived directly next door, I began to trust her and share more of my personal life with her. She knew Julie was a difficult child and that I struggled with parenting her. I even told her that she was seeing a psychologist.

Over the next few months, I could feel things changing. One evening after she and her daughter had eaten dinner with us, Julie and her daughter (ages 5 and 3) peed on the bathroom floor. I talked to Julie after she left and she said the little girl had an accident and she didn't want her to get into trouble so she peed too. I knew it sounded strange and Julie definitely had impulse control problems, but I didn't think it was a huge deal. The next day the woman came over and said that she and her husband were terribly upset and that their daughter was no longer allowed to play with Julie.

When I spoke to her later, she told me that she thought Julie was a "bad seed." She said if I spent more time doing things with her instead of taking her to psychologists that maybe she would be a better kid. She told me that she didn't like Julie and wanted me to help her keep the two girls apart.

Before I knew it, Julie was the black sheep of the block. Whatever happened was always her fault. The news of her being a "bad kid" was being spread. She wasn't allowed in our neighbor's home and we began to feel very isolated. I couldn't let her play outside alone for fear of how she would be treated by the other parents, and, of course, her behavior started to deteriorate as well. She began more frequent tantrums and many times would stand in her window at the front of the house screaming and banging on the windows.

We had originally left our two yards connected so the children could play freely back and forth. One day I looked outside and saw a fence being installed. Another day, I came home with my children only to drive up on a birthday party for their little girl outside in the cul-de-sac. All the neighborhood children were invited except mine. There was a clown and lots of people milling about. It was awful trying to explain to my children why they couldn't go out and join them.

After a few more incidents like these, I began to realize that we could not raise our children in this environment. We had only lived in our home less than three years and we knew it would be a tremendous financial burden, but we had to get out. We had to live in a place where our children could be children and where Julie could have a fresh start. A "For Sale" sign went up in the yard within a few days, and three weeks later we sold it.

After the house went up for sale a couple of the neighbors told me that they were sorry and felt bad about what had occurred. I will never understand how people can stand by and allow things like this to happen. Why didn't anyone stand up for what was right? I felt like they knew me and the kind of person I was. I really believed they would do the right thing, but they didn't. They took the easy choice of going along with the crowd. I hope if I am ever in that type of situation, I am stronger and make a better decision.

The good news is that our new home has been wonderful. We are so much happier and our kids are accepted and liked. I know I am much more cautious now. It took me a long time to trust again. I'm told I was quite aloof when we first moved in. We now feel like part of our community again.

"I can't even imagine what my neighbors must think. There are times when Carrie screams so loud, I know they can hear her. One time when I had sent her to her room for a time out and I was working in the front yard, she came to her bedroom window, which faced the front of the house, and started banging on the window and screaming. She was yelling how much she hated me. She looked truly 'mad.' The neighbors were pretty distant after that." (Nancy)

"Our friends have stopped inviting us over or out to dinner with our kids. I've turned offers down so often or left early after Conner lost control that no one wants to bother anymore. I can't blame them. I try to have parties at our house once in a while so lots of friends can get together all at the same time. That way, if my family has trouble, there are other people to talk with, other kids to deal with, and other things to talk about. Conner also feels more comfortable so he's better behaved." (Eileen)

ACTIVITIES YOU CAN DO AS A FAMILY

Finding activities that your family can do together is another aspect of your life that will continue to be affected by having a Bipolar child. While your friends might try to avoid taking their very young child to a place where he needs to be quiet, sit still, be on his best behavior, and follow the rules, they can occasionally attempt it. Their child might misbehave a bit, and they might be on edge the whole time, but it can be done. As their child gets older, it gets easier and easier to go to nice restaurants, to a live show or some other event that isn't specifically designed for children. Your Bipolar child, no matter what the age, may struggle if he's expected to sit in a quiet, structured setting. Consequently, your choice of family activities may end up seeming to revolve around your Bipolar child.

You and your partner might end up taking turns going to one activity or another with your other children or with your friends because those events just aren't suitable for your Bipolar child. That's a natural way of dealing with your situation. There's nothing wrong with it—in fact it's a good strategy to make sure your other children get to go where they want and need to go. It just doesn't promote family togetherness when everyone is going in different directions.

Instead of giving up on being together as a family, consciously choose activities that are realistic for your family. There are many things your family can do together. Most of the activities that will be fun for your Bipolar child will also be fun for your other children. You might walk away with a headache from some of them, but it will probably be worth it to have done something positive with the whole family.

Look for situations that:

▲ Don't require your child to be quiet for long periods of time

▲ Don't require lots of social skills

▲ Provide opportunities for your child to be energetic

▲ Have lots of external stimuli that will attract and keep your child's attention

▲ Have opportunities to shift attention from one thing to another

These suggestions might seem strange to someone who doesn't have experience with a Bipolar child because it seems like these types of situations would just get them overexcited. In reality, though, when there is external excitement, Bipolar kids tend to do better. They like the drama, the freedom, and the diversity that these situations provide.

Some outings that fit this description include:

▲ Children's museum with many hands-on activities

▲ Pay for play restaurant, such as Chuck E. Cheese's

▲ Arcade (If your child has a hard time with losing, this might not be a great idea for him.)

▲ Amusement park (Spinning rides tend to be calming for Bipolar kids.)

▲ Live theater for children

▲ Movies for children (This only works if the movie is age-appropriate and is something that your child definitely wants to see. It's best to have another adult with you so, if your Bipolar child needs to leave the theater for a while, someone else can stay with your other children.)

▲ Swimming pool, lake, ocean

▲ Playground (Try to find one that isn't overcrowded. This activity can stress your child's social skills if she has to interact a lot while she's playing on the equipment.)

▲ Cooking project (If it's too hard for your Bipolar child to stay focused through the whole project, have different kids do different parts of the project. They all will have contributed to an outcome they can enjoy together and you'll all be in the same room, involved in the same activity.)

"My kids and I had a great time baking for the holidays. All my kids were excited about sharing what they had created with the rest of the family. Not only did they have a great sense of accomplishment, but we had several hours together in the kitchen without anybody having a temper tantrum or fight. Sure, frequent licks of chocolate and frosting helped keep them interested, but I can't remember the last time we were happily together for so long. This will be a great memory for all of us." (Marjorie)

▲ Picnic

▲ Roller or ice skating at a rink

▲ Family bike ride or hike

Even if you've picked what should be the right type of activity, we all know that even the best-laid plans don't always go the way they are meant to. For parents of a Bipolar child, this may be the case more often than not. If things start to get difficult, find a way to separate your Bipolar child from the activity. Go to the car, a restroom or just a separate area. If he knows he's missing out on what everyone else is doing, he might have enough incentive to behave better. If he's not able to do that, everyone else in the family will at least have had a little extra time to have fun, as well as a warning that they may have to leave soon. This is especially important if you have other kids who might end up feeling extremely resentful if they always have to stop doing something fun the instant their sibling starts having trouble.

♥ *Sometimes, no matter how hard I try to make things nice and special, things just don't go well. Unfortunately, many times it is impossible to predict. Julie was so excited to take this hike that I had done many times as a child. I thought it would be a great experience but she just got into one of those moods where nothing was right. Her shoes didn't feel good, the water didn't taste right, she was hungry and didn't like what we had brought, she was tired, her legs hurt . . . Anyway, I ended up carrying her about half of the way piggy-back style. I got a great workout, but I could hardly walk the next two days.*

FAMILY PLANNING

If you already have other children and you know you don't want more, or you already know your Bipolar child will be your only child, you don't have to worry about planning for additional children. If you had planned on having more children, however, family planning can become a big issue once you find out your child has Bipolar Disorder. If it happened once, it can happen again. Even if it doesn't, having one Bipolar child can feel like having many children. Do you have the time and energy to take care of another child, whether or not he or she has a brain disorder?

You are certainly not alone in your worries. Many parents of Bipolar children wonder about how family life and parenting will be with another child. They also wonder whether they'll be doing their existing child(ren) a disservice if they have another child. Some even wonder whether they'll be doing a future child a disservice by bringing him or her into a family that is affected by Bipolar Disorder. Some of the other difficult thoughts that arise when you're thinking about family planning can be extremely hard to acknowledge. Who wants to admit that she has wondered if maybe it would have been better if her Bipolar child had never been born? No one really wants to blame her partner for having a family history of disorders that might affect future children. No one wants to feel resentful that her Bipolar child's needs are having yet another major impact on the family.

All of these thoughts are perfectly normal. There is no right or wrong. Try not to feel guilty about having them. Instead, explore whatever your true feelings are. Try to put your concerns into words and share them with your partner so you can come to a comfortable decision together.

While you're considering your options, remember that you are not going through this alone. Parents of children who are just difficult but not diagnosed with a brain disorder, parents of children with congenital physical defects, and parents of children with other hereditary illnesses go through this, too. Even parents of perfectly normal children change their minds about how many children to have once they've found out that the concept of having kids is very different than the reality of having them. When you look at it, very few families turn out exactly as planned.

♥   *Julie was such a difficult baby and toddler that I couldn't even begin to imagine having another child. My friends were starting to have more children and I watched as they learned to manage the needs of more than one child. I was barely managing to do anything for myself or my husband let alone another child. On top of the sheer workload, I was terrified that I would have another baby like Julie and didn't know if I could handle it. I delayed having a second child until Julie was in a special school and was having a somewhat stable period. I thought I'd better do it then or the space between my kids would be too big. It was strange planning my second pregnancy mostly around what was going on with Julie, but, to be honest, everything got planned around Julie.*

"There have been many times that I ask myself whether it was fair to me or the girls to have had them. I adore them, but my oldest child is like having 3 children already. Thank goodness they are too young to notice how much attention goes to their big brother. I worry about how they're going to feel about it when they're older. I hope that things will be easier by the time I have to explain it to them." (Yvonne)

"I've seen what psychiatric disorders did to my uncle's and brother's lives. I feel incredibly guilty about passing a bad gene along to my daughter, but we didn't realize at the time that my relative's bizarre behavior was a hereditary disorder. Now that we know she has Bipolar Disorder, it's difficult to have another baby when I feel like we'd be passing along a ticking time bomb." (Tom)

11
Handling the Financial Aspects of Having a Bipolar Child

In addition to going to extremes to provide medical and psychiatric care for your child, handle the many ways in which having a Bipolar child affects you and your family, and support your child through the fluctuations in her moods, Bipolar Disorder will force you to expend a huge amount of financial resources on your child. Managing the family's finances to ensure that you have the ability to take care of every family member—now and in the future—is one of the most tangible and important responsibilities of being a parent.

INSURANCE-RELATED STRATEGIES

As you've probably realized by now, doctors and medications are going to be an on-going, necessary part of your child's life, and, therefore, yours as well. With childhood-onset Bipolar Disorder, you are dealing with a growing child who is constantly facing new developmental, social and physical changes. Just when you think you've got the medication types and dosages figured out, something will change and your child will need more or a different type of therapy and/or medication adjustments. Bipolar Disorder requires expensive professional and pharmacological assistance. It doesn't get fixed and go away. As costly as it can be to find and use the appropriate medical services for your child, there really is no alternative since your child will likely continue to need medications and therapy.

Dealing with insurance coverage is going to be one key factor in your financial management strategy. Even for families with the best insurance coverage and a strong financial base, Bipolar Disorder can put a huge drain on a family's resources. For families with low to moderate income or less than wonderful insurance, it can create incredible financial stress. While it's certainly appropriate to make choices to help you balance all the family's financial needs, treatment of your child's disorder will be a top priority. If Bipolar Disorder isn't successfully treated, it most likely will get worse and worse, affecting not just your finances, but also the relationships, health and happiness of your whole family.

Your challenge is going to be obtaining the best possible services for your child, while causing your family the least financial distress. Since every family's financial and insurance situation is different, this chapter offers some general strategies to help you navigate the maze of policies, legislation and procedures that affect private and public insurance coverage. A critical factor to keep in mind is that while Bipolar Disorder is considered a mental illness, it is a biologically-based health issue. Therefore, according to recent legislation, it must receive the same coverage that any other type of medical problem would. Of course, unless you strongly remind service providers and insurance companies of this important aspect of Bipolar Disorder, they may try to treat it as a mental health condition that has much more limited coverage.

Avoiding Insurance Problems:

Following are some specific steps you can take to minimize the amount of insurance hassles you will have to face. Again, information is power. The more you know how to manage the system, the easier and more successful it should be.

▲ Ask the employer who's providing your insurance coverage if you have the option to purchase and pay for additional coverage that would help you care for your child, such as prescription coverage.

▲ Know the state and federal regulations that affect insurance coverage for treatment of Bipolar Disorder before there's a problem.

Sometimes you can avoid or minimize problems just by letting medical and insurance providers know how educated you are and how you will fight to get the coverage you are entitled to. You can find this information by contacting your state board of insurance or by going online. Use the words "biologically based mental" to start your search.

▲ Use doctors, hospitals, pharmacists and other healthcare providers who are covered by your insurance company. Before you use someone, check with the insurance company to make sure they are on the list. Then, check with the provider to make sure they plan to stay with that insurance company.

▲ Whenever possible, go to doctors who complete and file the insurance claims for you. Not only will it be easier, but you won't have to pay up front, then wait for reimbursement later from the insurance company.

Dealing with Insurance Companies:

▲ Many HMO's require you to choose a Primary Care Physician. You must see your Primary Care Physician initially. That doctor then determines if you need to see a specialist, including mental healthcare providers. This process can be extremely tedious, time consuming, and expensive, but it's necessary. So, it's extremely important to select a primary care physician who won't be stingy with his/her referrals.

▲ Track every medical situation. List the date, nature of the service, the name(s) of the provider(s), the specific tests/assessments that were performed, and the possible or actual diagnoses. Also keep a copy of each report about your child.

▲ Track every single insurance claim. Keep a copy of anything you send to the insurance company. Make sure everything is dated.

▲ Keep track of the payments you receive. Check them against the claims that you submitted. This will make it much easier to track what claims have and have not been paid and to resubmit claims when necessary.

▲ When you have to contact the insurance company, ask for and write down the name of the person to whom you speak. Ask for the correct spelling of that person's name so he/she knows you are keeping a record of the conversation. Also write down what was discussed and what the insurance representative said. Do this each time, not just when you have problems.

▲ If you discuss something particularly important with the insurance company, especially if you are told that if you do one thing then they will do another, it's a good idea to put everything in writing. Send or fax a letter to confirm the details. Be sure to list the specific claim you are referencing and the information and instructions from the insurance representative, whose name you should include. Once your understanding of the situation is in writing, it's harder for them to argue the issue later if they didn't follow up immediately after receiving your letter.

▲ If you find someone at the insurance company who tends to be very helpful, easy to work with, and understanding, ask for his/her direct number. Mention that you appreciate his/her assistance and wonder if you can contact him/her directly the next time you need to call the company.

▲ When you're on the phone with an insurance company, it's normal to be transferred from one person to another. Ask for the name and number of the person to whom you are being transferred so you can call back directly if you happen to get disconnected or sent to the wrong person.

▲ Get a copy of your full policy. You can get it directly from the insurance company or, if it's provided by an employer, from the human resource department. Study it so you are familiar with exactly what is and isn't covered. If you have questions, contact the insurance company for clarification.

▲ You need to know the following about your insurance coverage:

  ▲ What the yearly and lifetime limits are for medical care: remember, Bipolar Disorder qualifies as a biologically-based mental illness so it has the same limitations and coverage as any other illness. (i.e. the limits on coverage for mental illness do not apply)

▲ What doctors, hospitals, pharmacies and mental healthcare providers are in the plan

▲ Whether or not you have any coverage if you go to a doctor outside of the network and, if so, what percent is covered

▲ How referrals must be made

▲ What pre-authorizations are required for hospitalization, tests or procedures

▲ What medications are not covered and, if there is a generic form of a medication, whether or not the name brand is still covered

▲ What types of services are not covered (such as substance abuse treatment or residential programs)

▲ What constitutes an "emergency" when you can hospitalize your child without pre-authorization

▲ Carefully evaluate your insurance options. What seems more expensive initially may end up saving you money in the long run.

▲ Prescriptions tend to be one of the more expensive aspects of caring for a child with Bipolar Disorder. Even if your child is only taking a few medications, your monthly costs without insurance coverage could be well over $100. Adding new medications or making medication changes could easily make that much, much higher. Research prescription plans through a medical insurance company, private prescription plans, and social services.

▲ Some drug companies offer patient assistance programs to help cover the cost of medications when insurance coverage has run out. Ask the pharmacist for the name of the manufacturers of your child's medications if you want to contact them for information on these types of programs.

"We got sick and tired of jumping through the insurance company's hoops. We would have had to wait weeks to get our daughter in to see a psychiatrist. We were in crisis and just couldn't deal with that. We decided to get Sophia

in to see a doctor with a great reputation for his diagnostic skills and just pay for it out of our own pockets. We'll deal with the insurance for the ongoing therapy." (Kris)

Dealing with Doctors:

▲ Ask for a free initial consultation when considering a new doctor. Not all doctors will do this for free, but it's always worth a try.

▲ When a doctor is making a referral or writing a prescription, notify him/her of your insurance coverage requirements and limits. Encourage her to consider your coverage when making choices. Of course, if what's best for your child isn't covered, you're the one who will have to make a choice about whether to pay for it yourself or try the next best, covered option.

▲ Ask your doctor for as many prescription samples as he/she's willing to provide. He/she may be able to give you a few samples at each visit.

▲ If you have a prescription policy, ask your doctor to write a prescription for the largest number of pills possible at a time. It's much better, for example, to pay $20 for 100 pills than $20 for 50!

▲ Remind the doctor to make it clear in the information submitted to the insurance company that the treatment, prescription, or cause of the problem is Bipolar Disorder. Because the law requires parity in the treatment of biologically-based mental illness (meaning it has to receive the same coverage as any other physical disorder), having the Bipolar diagnosis will help you get the level of coverage you deserve, rather than the limited coverage that applies to other types of mental illness. Even if the doctor is treating other symptoms, such as attention deficit, if he diagnoses it as part of Bipolar Disorder, rather than as a separate, non-biologically-based disorder, you will get better insurance coverage.

▲ Some prescription plans charge very similar prices for different dosages of medications. Ask your doctor to help you find the cheapest way to get the medications. For example, you might be able to get higher dose pills that can be cut in half for two different doses.

Finding and Choosing Medical Insurance:

If you have an opportunity to choose new insurance coverage, evaluate the factors listed below. Weigh them against the costs of the premiums.

▲ What is the deductable?

▲ How much do you have to pay out-of-pocket for each doctor visit?

▲ What, if any, prescriptions are covered? How much? What is the co-payment?

▲ What hospitals are included in the plan?

▲ Are referrals needed in order for you to visit a specialist?

▲ What limits, if any, apply to general medical coverage?

▲ What limits apply to inpatient and outpatient mental healthcare? (just in case your child needs treatment specifically for other mental health conditions that are not biologically-based)

▲ How large is the list of doctors covered through the plan?

▲ If only certain doctors are covered, is any amount paid to doctors out of the network?

▲ Ask the benefits coordinator for the employer that's providing the plan whether there are other options that might suit your needs better.

▲ Some membership groups, such as chambers of commerce, professional organizations, and trade associations offer group insurance plans. It might be worth your while to join one!

▲ There may come a time when it is appropriate to choose employment based on the type of insurance they offer. Typically, your best bet will be a larger employer since companies with fewer than 50 employees are exempt from many aspects of healthcare legislation that affect insurance coverage. Other good bets are companies that are unionized or have many offices around the country. It's okay to contact the benefits coordinator of the company to ask about the types of insurance options they provide.

▲ Many states offer public "insurance" coverage programs for uninsured children and/or low-income families. Contact your state department of social or health services for information and assistance. The U.S. Department of Health and Human Services website also has information about insurance programs for uninsured kids. (Please see the *Additional Resources* section for websites and phone numbers.)

Dealing with Insurance Problems:

So, you've done everything right, but the insurance company denies a claim. Or, maybe you didn't, but you still think that coverage should be provided. The reality is that no matter how you handle insurance claims, insurance companies make a lot of denials. Be prepared to challenge each and every one. There are some specific and important steps you can take to get what you deserve. While the process seems simple and straightforward, it can get complicated and extremely frustrating.

▲ If you don't like how the insurance company handles a claim, submit a formal appeal in writing. Put the word "grievance" at the top. This makes your letter a legal document, not just a note. The insurance company has to respond to it. Include a detailed description of the reasons why you think they should be paying the claim. Whenever possible refer to specific sections of the insurance policy. If appropriate, reference the notes that you've taken and discussions you've had with insurance claims representatives. Send the letter to the claims representative and a copy to a senior manager. (Get a name from the claims representative with whom you've been working or just call the company receptionist to get the proper name.) Make sure to keep a copy.

▲ If the insurance company turns you down again and you still feel that you have a legitimate claim, appeal again and again.

▲ If the situation continues to be a problem, write a letter to your state insurance board or commission. You can find the address in the phone directory in the state government section of your white pages. Send a copy to the insurance company and continue to urge them to change their decision.

▲ If you get your insurance through your employer, ask the employee assistance program or benefits coordinator to contact the insurance company regarding your issue. The insurance company might be more willing to work with you if your employer contacts them because they won't want to risk losing the company's business.

▲ Try to control your anger and frustration. Try to get the claim representative on your side. Ask his/her opinion on how you should handle the situation. Explain how urgent or important the need is and convey that he/she is helping you care for your child. Remind him/her that delaying treatment or providing less than is necessary now, might result in more costly and prolonged treatment being needed later.

▲ Ask a lot of questions. Obtain and document as much information as possible about why the insurance company is making the decisions they're making.

▲ When necessary, refer to or send a copy of the Bipolar Disorder description in the *DSM-IV*, the medical manual that provides diagnostic criteria. This will reinforce that Bipolar Disorder is a biologically-based disorder that by law must receive the same insurance coverage as any other medical disorder. (You can find the *DSM-IV* online, at the library, or at a doctor's office.)

FINANCIAL STRATEGIES

Your role as a parent probably will extend long beyond the traditional eighteen years. Your worries about your child's current struggles must not stop you from doing what you have to do now to protect your own, your family's, and your child's future. Even though your day-to-day caretaking may be so intense that you can hardly think about the future, you do have to plan wisely for it now, while managing the on-going care of everyone in the family. Planning for the future is a critical step in ensuring that your child, as well as the rest of your family, has sufficient financial support for the coming years.

Even if you rationally know that you should be saving some money for dealing with future Bipolar care or for your own retirement, it's not easy to just pull the plug on treatment and say, "That's all we can afford to do right now" when your child is in crisis. That's why it's important to have a variety of financial strategies in place to help you protect and manage your financial resources. These plans should include retirement savings plans, life insurance, long-term care insurance and/or other financial tools to protect your financial resources as much as possible. These strategies will also help you make sure that if something happens to you, your child will have some financial resources to take care of himself and continue his care.

You can obtain some of the information you'll need on the Internet, but it takes a lot of time and energy to research each individual option. It's also hard to compare one plan to another. It's a good idea to do some general on-line research, but the help of insurance, financial, and legal experts will help you make better choices, faster. When it comes to getting advice, talk to several different financial professionals, preferably brokers who represent a variety of financial products, who will help you evaluate how well different options suit your particular situation. Remember, you can meet with many different professionals before you make any choices. You're the client. Let them sell you on their particular services.

▲ While medical insurance is critical for parents of Bipolar children, that's not the only type of insurance that can help. It might be appropriate, for example, to adjust your homeowner's liability insurance to cover harm or destruction your child might cause.

▲ Some states have specific tax deductions that apply to families with disabled children. Check with a tax accountant for specific information.

▲ Talk to a tax accountant about the possibility of setting up a pre-tax medical spending account. When you pay medical bills with pre-tax dollars, it ends up costing you much less.

▲ Keep track of every single expense related to treating your child. This includes mileage to doctor's appointments, gas, and parking in addition to the actual costs of medical care, therapy and medication. Almost all of it is tax deductible.

▲ If your family is low to moderate income, take advantage of every program for which you qualify. Subsidized or free school lunches are one option. Contact your county department of social or health services for assistance.

▲ Your child might be able to qualify for Supplemental Security Income payments. This program pays cash to cover basic living expenses for low-income families with a disabled child. (Psychologically disabled counts!) Contact your local social security office for details. (We warn you, though. It can be a long and difficult process to first find someone who can help you as well as to actually qualify for payments.) Look in the government section of the white pages directory for the phone number. For more information, you can also go to the Supplemental Security Income section of the Social Security Administration website. (See the *Additional Resources* section.)

▲ Get the best life insurance you can afford for you and for your partner. This will give your child a cushion in case he can't fully support himself when he's older and you're gone.

▲ Get life insurance on your child if you can afford it. This may be very difficult to think about. You might feel that you don't want to "benefit" from your child's death, but life insurance proceeds can pay for funeral expenses, cover therapy for you and your other family members to cope with the trauma, and "pay back" the accounts that were run down in order to pay for your child's care. There's nothing wrong with it.

▲ Make a formal, legal will that names a guardian for your child. Make sure the person you name is aware of your choice and is willing to accept that responsibility in the event that something happens to you.

▲ Evaluate whether it's appropriate to set up a trust to protect money for your child. This trust might last into adulthood. This gives you the opportunity to name a trustee who can help your child, even when she's an adult, make wise financial choices. You can also name someone to make medical decisions on your child's behalf if she isn't competent to do so.

▲ Consider obtaining long-term care insurance for yourself, your partner and possibly even your child. This type of insurance can cover in-home or nursing home-type care for people who cannot move, feed, dress, and/or bathe themselves. For parents in particular, this is a strategy to help ensure that you'll be well cared for should you ever require help, but you've used all your financial resources on your child's care or your child isn't able to care for you. These plans pay for long-term care due to any cause, not just old age.

EXTREME OPTIONS

Sometimes, there just isn't any way for a family to obtain and pay for the type of services their child needs. In these extreme situations, some families have gone so far as to give up custody of their children so that those children could obtain free, public services. Other parents have divorced so one could quality for services for low income or indigent parents. These parents have given up a lot in order to provide for their children in they only way they knew how. In some ways, recent legislation, improved understanding of mental illness, and formal definition of Bipolar Disorder as a biologically- based mental disorder will help other parents avoid these drastic measures. However, recent changes to the welfare system have made it even more difficult for low-income families to obtain the on-going, long-term care needed for Bipolar Disorder.

Before you go to extreme measures to obtain care for your Bipolar child, such as temporarily giving up custody of your child to the Department of Social Services so that your child's care can be covered by Medicaid, make sure you have exhausted all other possibilities. Once you take steps to change custody, financial status or marital status, you might limit other options, find that you can't change your mind, or find that you no longer have any say in your child's care. If you do decide that your child requires more extensive treatment than you or your insurance company can provide, contact your county's office of the Department of Social Services. They can help you evaluate your options related to publicly-funded services.

"It became clear to me and my daughter's psychiatrist that she needed long-term, constant, professional care in order to make sure she stayed safe and learned to control her behavior. When we talked to the insurance company, they made it very clear that if she were bleeding in the emergency room from

self-inflicted wounds, they would authorize short-term hospitalization, but that my coverage didn't include long-term care to make sure she never got to that point. I was desperate. I knew I had to do something drastic if I wanted to save my child from herself. After a heart-wrenching meeting with the Department of Social Services, I decided that my only option was to sign a Voluntary Dependency and Neglect order, which gave them temporary custody of Ellisa. They supported the psychiatrist's recommendation to place her in a residential treatment facility, but I was shocked to find that she had to go out of state. Some impossibly ridiculous capitation rules mean that a residential facility gets more money for out of state patients than in-state patients. Instead of sending her to a local facility that I had visited and found to be wonderful, she was sent halfway across the country. The therapists say they encourage family visits and involvement, but how can I do that when the whole reason that I gave up custody was that I couldn't afford to pay for her treatment? I can't afford to live nearby for the 9-12 months that she will be there! While they do contact me on a regular basis, report on Ellisa's progress, and ask my opinions, I know that I am not in control anymore. I can't wait until she is safe and stable enough that I can get custody back and bring her home. I pray that I don't have any trouble getting custody back." (Shelly)

"There is no way we can afford to pay over $700 per day for 5 days or so of hospitalization and over $400 per day for about a year of residential treatment. There is also no way that we can keep our child from hurting himself and others. We're practically bankrupt from paying for years of therapy as it is. Whether it's divorcing or giving up custody so Matthew qualifies for Medicaid, I guess we have to at least consider it." (Yvonne)

"If I have to sell my house, my car and my jewelry in order to pay for Payton's treatment, I will do that before I give up custody of my child. I just know that no one can make better choices for her than I can. If we can't afford hospitalization, we just won't do it. I'll spend every minute of the day with her before I'll send her away." (Terryn)

GUARDIANSHIP

Unfortunately, even if you've organized your finances to prepare for the worst, it still sometimes happens. Unforeseen circumstances can affect your actual ability to parent your Bipolar child. Because of the intensity involved in this type of parenting, it's extremely important that you take the appropriate steps to formally appoint a legal guardian in the event that something happens to you. Think about who would most likely parent your child in the same manner that you would parent him. Make sure to select somebody who is emotionally, intellectually and, if you won't be leaving a substantial inheritance behind, financially able to care for your child. Also make sure that this person agrees to accept the responsibility and that there is a legal document that names the guardian. Keep in mind that the person most appropriate to be the guardian of your child when he's young might not be right if he or she inherits the role when your child is a teenager. You'll want to periodically review and update your will as your child changes and grows.

SECTION FIVE:

Taking Care of Yourself

12
Managing Bipolar Disorder's Effects on Your Marriage

PARENTING TOGETHER

You and your spouse have already been through incredible amounts of stress worrying about your child, trying to find help, getting a diagnosis, and making difficult decisions about treatment. If you've worked together and shared not just information about Bipolar Disorder but also your feelings about how it affects your child and your own lives, if you've been understanding and helpful when one or the other gets overwhelmed, you are doing better than most couples. If you haven't, the going isn't likely to get that much easier over time. You can't change the fact that you have a Bipolar child, but you can take the time to re-establish a mutually beneficial and supportive relationship. A good place to start is evaluating both your roles as partners and as parents. How are those roles defined now? What is and is not working? What feels OK and what doesn't?

When you've cared for your relationship as partners, you may find that it's easier to jointly perform your responsibilities as parents. Of course, there might be times that you disagree on discipline strategies, medical treatment, medication, or other aspects of dealing with your child's Bipolar Disorder, but it will be easier to communicate with each other and come to joint decisions if your relationship is strong. If you can't come to mutual agreement, though, you can't let that stop you from treating your child. One of you is going to have to be the primary caregiver, with the authority to make medical decisions, and the other one is going to have to allow that to happen. What's more, the partner who isn't making the medical decisions has to support those choices, through both words and actions, if the treatment is to help your child. The term "putting up a united front" is apt in this situation. Inconsistency and arguments will only make matters worse.

It is a common frustration for parents to have different perspectives on how to take care of their Bipolar child. It's normal for one parent to become the primary caregiver for the Bipolar child, just as in typical families one parent is the primary caregiver even if both work. (Since the mom is usually the primary caregiver, we'll use female pronouns for that parent and male pronouns for the other parent. All the information can work either way, however.) That parent often wishes that her spouse would be more involved in the care, more supportive, and give more recognition of the effort and stresses involved in providing that care. The parent who isn't as involved may develop strong beliefs about how things should be handled and/or have feelings of resentment that seemingly all the attention is going to the children. Just as teachers don't always see all the Bipolar symptoms, spouses often don't get the brunt of it. They may not even see it or totally believe it.

> *"Yesterday, for the first time, my son pulled his act with his father. I was so happy to see it happen to him and not just me for a change. Maybe now my husband will start to understand why I can't pay attention to him when our son is having a Bipolar episode."* (Julianna)

BEING PARTNERS, NOT JUST PARENTS

Unfortunately, it's often difficult, in the midst of dealing with screaming rages, broken furniture, visits to doctors, and everything else that goes along with having a Bipolar child, to stop and focus on your own needs as couple. Of course, this is hard for many parents, but particularly difficult in the case of families affected by Bipolar Disorder. Even if we know that we deserve to have the time and energy to take care of ourselves and our partners, it's hard to justify taking that time and energy when our child needs it so much. Nevertheless, if you want to stay in a strong relationship (we will use the term marriage, but this information applies to any couple), you have to make an effort to take care of your marriage while you're taking care of your Bipolar child. If you can't seem to justify focusing on your own needs, including the need to take care of your marriage, remind yourself that the happier you are, the better you can care for your child. In addition, keep in mind that having a strong, supportive relationship with your partner is not only a key factor in being fulfilled as a person, it is also one of the most important gifts you can give a Bipolar child. A lasting marriage will help satisfy your child's strong need for continuity, control and a stable home life. Even when things are extremely difficult between partners, make the effort for yourselves as well as for your child.

It's very easy for both parents to end up being so upset over issues that relate to their child that they ignore or forget issues that relate to just themselves. Your spouse should be the backbone of your support system, but this takes work and constant communication. He should also be all the other things you want from your life partner: a friend, a companion, a lover, and a confidant. If you look at the national divorce rate you will see that marriage even without the added difficulties we face is extremely difficult. We cannot make our marriages our last priority, which is incredibly easy to do when you are dealing with so many other intense issues on a daily basis. It is so important to nurture, value and invest in our marriages.

Even if it feels like you are forcing yourself initially, talk to, spend time with and make love to your spouse regularly. Make sure he feels loved and appreciated. It may not seem possible now, but there will come a time when your children are more independent and more on their own. You will be left with your spouse once the kids leave home . . . make sure he/she will not be a stranger. Even on those days when it feels like the last thing you want to do or have the energy to do, try to relax, shift gears, and spend some time being with your spouse. You'll probably find that it makes you feel better to change from being a parent to being a partner and adult for a while.

Paying more attention to your spouse may also open the door for him to feel like being more involved in caring for your child and being supportive of your efforts. It might feel like giving in at first—once again you're having to do what someone else needs you to do before you can get what you need—but you have to make a decision. Is the outcome important enough to justify the means? Knowing that you'll likely get a good outcome may help you feel less resentful about being the first one to do what the other spouse needs.

"Cindy and I had Julie 10 years ago, on Christmas day 1990. We were so excited about being new parents, and anticipating the joy of having our own baby. As I look back at those first three days in the hospital, I realize that we had no idea what was in store for us. Ten long years have passed, and as we coped with our daughter, we neglected ourselves, and our marriage. The intensity of our situation, and the attention that Julie required, sent me into a controlled seclusion. As Cindy constantly cared for Julie, I took on the role of the provider. As time passed and our marriage deteriorated, I had no idea what was happening. I had built a wall up around me. Now I struggle to save the one thing that was so important before this all started, and that is the woman I love. Remember to treat your wife as an individual, not an extension of your troubled child. Show her you care, and offer as much of yourself as you can to help her in raising your child. Make the time you have alone with your spouse special, and let her know that what she does is important. You only have one chance to live your life the way you and your spouse always dreamed, make each moment count, even the stressful ones."
(Jeff)

"I have no time for my husband or myself. I miss the old me and my husband misses her too. I wish I could get her back, but I know I'll never be the same. I feel lost, a shadow of my former self." (Zenia)

"I feel like all my husband and I ever talk about is Justin. Even when he calls me during the day from work, I'm usually so upset that I talk about it then, too. I don't have the energy to even care about what is going on in his life. It's hard enough just being me, I can't imagine having to be married to me." (Tonya)

"There are days I'm not sure I'll make it. Will my marriage survive this kind of stress? What is this doing to my other children? How can I do this one more day, let alone the rest of my life?" (Chris)

Even if you're both really trying, but especially if one of you isn't, marriage counseling can be a great help. Talk to other couples, your regular doctor, your child's doctors, and your insurance company to find someone with whom you can both relate and who understands the special stresses involved in your marriage. You can use a lot of the strategies described in Chapter Three to help you find and use a good therapist.

Once again, it's extremely difficult to admit that you have a situation that is causing a lot of trouble and that you can't fix it on your own. It's also similar to obtaining and dealing with the Bipolar diagnosis in that you'll have to focus on someone else's needs and moods and behaviors. With a marriage, unlike with parenting, the reality is that you do have a choice about how much effort you want to invest. You can opt out. Just remember that deciding not to work on strengthening your marriage brings with it a whole bunch of other, difficult situations and emotions. Keep reading.

WHEN PARENTS AREN'T PARTNERS

Looking at the national divorce rate is dismal enough, but adding the stress of a special needs child brings the risk up even higher. So, it is not unfair to assume that many parents of children with Bipolar Disorder will think about, discuss, and experience divorce.

It's no surprise that many of our marriages do not survive. One parent typically ends up handling doctors' appointments, homework, discipline, medications, and other daily activities. If the other parent isn't involved in these activities, he can begin to feel very inadequate at handling the child. As a result, he can begin to defer responsibility more and more to his spouse. In return, the parent acting as the primary caregiver begins to feel alone, angry and resentful, often placing the brunt of the exhaustion, frustration and anger that accompanies caring for the child on her partner.

As if divorce was not scary enough in it's own right, divorce with a Bipolar child in the mix is complicated and unpredictable at best. Parents of Bipolar children have all the same questions and issues to address as everyone else, but they also have a gamut of other important issues to work out and worry about as well.

"I don't know what to do. My marriage has deteriorated so badly. I really wish I could make a change but I am terrified. How will I take care of Jason alone? Could I possibly do it financially? How will I work and get him to all his appointments and be there for him on his bad days? Could my

husband even get him ready for school without me? What if he has a rage when he is at his father's? What is worse for him—living with parents in a bad marriage or going through the stress of a divorce? What if my husband has girlfriends or remarries and they are not kind to or accepting of Jason? Will I have less control over medical decisions?" (Jessica)

Parenting becomes even harder when you're not parenting together. Both parents, who were probably able to use the "divide and conquer" approach to some degree when they were together, will have to learn to handle all of their children at once without that backup extra hand and support from their partner. It's difficult for the parent who hasn't been the primary caregiver/disciplinarian/problem solver/medication manager to learn how to do it on his own, when the Bipolar child is with him. That parent will need to learn skills in handling mood fluctuations, medications, and daily living support.   It's terrifying for the primary caregiver to imagine how well (or poorly, as the case may be) the other parent is caring for the child when they're alone together.   This is especially true if one of the main reasons you split up was that the other parent wasn't supporting the treatment, participating in care or effectively parenting your Bipolar child. It's frustrating, after you've made a difficult decision to end your marriage to still have to negotiate, communicate, and interact with your ex-spouse.

♥ *I never thought I would end up divorced in a million years. I married the perfect man and led the perfect life—at least that's how it looked from the outside. My parents divorced when I was young and I swore I would never complicate my kids' lives in that way. But, after years of marriage counseling and disappointment and unhappiness, I finally felt like there was no other choice. I felt that my unhappiness had reached a level where it was directly affecting my ability to be the mother I wanted to be, the mother I NEEDED to be for my children. Working on my marriage was encompassing so much of my emotional energy and my self-esteem that I really was limited in what I had left to give to my children. Every day I wake up and look in the mirror and pray that I will be able to look at myself and know I am OK and know that my kids will be OK.*

"My husband has been so unsupportive in raising Daniel. I have felt so alone in this and so lonely. I have made every major decision alone, been to

every psychiatrist, psychologist, occupational therapist, pediatrician and school appointment alone. I felt like instead of being a partner and a help, my husband was just one more person in the house that I was responsible for taking care of. The weirdest part of it all is that even though I am alone now, I am so much less lonely than I was with him. It's so hard to share your life with someone who has truly and deeply disappointed you. It must be one of the worst feelings in the world to lose respect for the man you love because he can't be a good parent to your child. As scary as this all is/was, I have to believe that we will be all right. One thing I do know is that I am such a better parent than I was before. I have so much more to give to my children because I am not expending so much energy worrying about and/or trying to save a marriage that is failing." (Victoria)

No matter what your relationship is with your former spouse, your relationship as parents will hopefully continue, for the sake of your child(ren). You are going to have to work out ways to communicate with each other regarding medical decisions, discipline, and daily challenges. Whether you separate the duties and let one of you handle the medical aspects of your child's life or you manage it together, make sure you have clear lines of communication. It has to work smoothly so that you can react quickly when your child is in crisis, so that your child doesn't manipulate you both by telling you one thing and your former spouse another, and so that all the important information about your child's life, moods, behaviors and needs can be monitored.

"Jordan called me last night at 10:00 from her father's house. She was bored and wanted to know what she should do. I calmly suggested that she go to bed, since it was two hours past her bedtime. I asked her whether she'd taken her pills (which she was supposed to have taken at 6:00) and done her homework. She got mad at me and said that Dad hadn't told her to do it and that he says he makes the rules for her when she's at his house. Since he hadn't told her to what to do, she hadn't done anything. When her Dad got on the phone, his response to my anger was to tell me that I had no business telling him how to run his house. I reminded him that Jordan is not part of the house, she's his child, but that didn't seem to register. I keep telling myself that this kind of reaction is one of the reasons I divorced the bastard, but sometimes I think I might have just made things worse for Jordan." (Allyson)

"Heidi loves that we're divorced. She's purposefully leaving things at the other house, frequently calling and complaining to the parent that she's not with, and sharing intimate details about my life with her father. This is just a whole new game to her. She has no concept of how sad I am or that she's lost something important in her life." (Meredith)

"It's easier for me to just take care of Cameron on my own. My ex-wife just gets herself so caught up in her own issues that she can't handle anyone else's. Working out a schedule for visitation is just too much for her. She can visit when she wants, but our lives are much less complicated when I have sole custody." (Jack)

"I should be able to relax and enjoy the time I have alone when my son is at his father's house, but all I can do is worry and wait for my ex-husband to call to say that he can't handle him and ask me what he should do." (Yvette)

Some ways to make communication and caretaking easier and more consistent include:

▲ Have the divorce settlement explicitly dictate how parental responsibility will be handled, including how medical decisions will be made regarding your Bipolar child. It's best, even if you share parental responsibility, to have the court appoint one of you as the one responsible for medical care.

▲ Create a method to share information about the time that the child spent with each of you. Email and voice messaging are great because you can share information without actually having to talk.

▲ Be as consistent as possible with your parenting time schedule. Your child has a hard enough time with change. Make sure she knows exactly what to expect each day. Keep a calendar up with the schedule that she can check anytime she wants to. You may even want to keep one in her backpack if she needs to look at it while at school.

▲ Provide the school and the team of caregivers with explicit information on who is and isn't permitted to pick up your child, make decisions regarding your child, and provide instructions regarding your child. Keep the school informed of all the changes that are taking place and make sure they have all the different emergency numbers and the order in which they should be called.

▲ Define who pays for what. If you can't do it on your own, get the court involved. If it gets difficult for the parent who is making expensive school or medical decisions to agree with the parent who is responsible for paying for the outcomes of those decisions, consider setting up a monthly or annual fund for your child. Agree on the amount each of you will put in and how you will make decisions about how to use the funds. Being able to access money when you need it, make decisions within your budget, and avoid frequent arguments about money makes divorced parenting much easier. Not having to continuously ask for or hand money over to the ex-spouse can greatly reduce stress and conflict.

"I technically have the legal authority to make decisions regarding my daughter's medical care and education, but my ex-husband thinks that he shouldn't have to give me any more than the monthly child support payment. So, when our daughter has problems and needs to be in a special school or have special therapy that the insurance won't cover, I can make the decision to do whatever I feel is necessary—I just can't pay for it." (Cheyenne)

▲ Parenting is a privilege, not a right. If your child is in danger because of an ex-spouse's negligence or actions, do what you have to do to get your child out of the situation as quickly as possible. Write down each and every situation that you feel is inappropriate or dangerous, and then report them to your lawyer. There may come a point that your ex-spouse's parental responsibility rights and/or parenting time agreement need to be challenged.

13
Getting What You Need

You deserve personal health and happiness just as every person does. The fact that you're a parent—and a parent of a Bipolar child in particular—does not change that even though practically your whole life revolves around Bipolar Disorder. It dictates much of what you can and can't do and when you can do it. So much of your schedule is based on your child's needs that your work, your physical fitness, your diet, and many other aspects of your personal life will be affected. In fact, it might be helpful to think of parenting your Bipolar child as a job. Like any other job, you can't do it 100% of the time. You need to have breaks, vacations and performance bonuses!

In fact, because you have such extreme stresses in your life, and on such a regular basis, it's even more important for you to take care of yourself. If it's not reason enough to take care of yourself because you deserve it, tell yourself that the stronger, happier and more personally fulfilled you are, the more physical and emotional energy you'll have to take care of everyone else. It may seem like there's no time to take care of your own needs, but you have to make the time. Don't just wait for there to be a good time.

FRIENDSHIPS

Friendships are just as important for you as for your child. You can't just be friends with the parents of your children's friends, either. It's important to keep up your own personal friendships, too. You'll definitely find out who your true friends are when you have a Bipolar child. Some friends just may not be able to cope—with your child or with the intensity of your life. Since it takes too much energy trying to teach people to be good, understanding and supportive friends, focus on those people who are already ready and able to have a strong, real and mutually satisfying friendship.

♥ *In my heart, I always believed that other people defined friendship the same way as I did. I thought that if I could educate and give people insight about my child's differences, understanding and acceptance would follow. I believed people could look beyond the exterior appearances of Julie's behaviors and see what was really inside. I believed that people who claimed to love me would love my child, for she was part of "me." I believed others would return kindness with kindness and caring with caring.*

What I now know is that everything I believed is true! The trick is finding friends who are worthy of such beliefs. Good people, people who are capable of being true friends, are not as common as we would like. People who are not limited by prejudice, ignorance, and intolerance are precious and rare. I have been incredibly lucky to find friends in my life who have met and surpassed all these criteria. As a matter of fact, these are the people who showed me what it meant to be a true friend. These are people who have been there through it all, never wavering in their love and support. They were always a phone call away. They listened when I cried, complained, or just felt sorry for myself. They loved Julie even when she was not easy to love. They understood when I didn't call for a week or two, or forgot to ask about what was important in their lives. They loved me even when I forgot dates, birthdays, phone calls, parties. They loved me even when I didn't love myself. I am truly a better person for having these remarkable people in my life.

Unfortunately, it's not always easy to spot wonderful friends. I have learned to see the signs of the three no-nos: prejudice, ignorance, and intolerance. Consequently, I save both my daughter and myself unnecessary pain. I'm embarrassed to admit how long it took me and how many "friend mistakes" I made along the way. Now, the minute I see any of those not-so-wonderful qualities in a new person, I turn, run, and get as far away as possible. It's not my job to help them become accepting, educated and tolerant people.

You're dealing with so much, so often, that there will probably be times when you feel like getting all the stuff you've been dealing with off your chest. There are also times when someone may confide something very personal to you and you want to confide back. This is how parents, especially mothers, build relationships with each other. This is a very wonderful experience as long as it is with the right friend. Someone may seem very open and accepting, but the unfortunate truth is that people are very frightened of mental illness and very few people are truly educated about it. They may then think your child is dangerous or "crazy" and, especially if they have children, want to avoid him. There is also something very dangerous about giving someone a label for your child when they may or may not be able to keep that information confidential. Make sure the people with whom you share your deepest darkest thoughts are true, trustworthy friends or the experience of talking with them could leave you feeling worse rather than better.

> ♥   *Children with mental illnesses are very emotionally draining. We have only so much physical, emotional and spiritual energy to go around. I have learned that I can't spare a place in my life for people who consistently drain me of energy or people who do not support me or make me feel good about what I am doing. It sounds very simple, but it was a very hard thing for me to learn and it requires a lot of confidence in yourself and your capabilities as a parent. There are some people who fit into this category that you might not be able to eliminate from your life, like family, teachers, or neighbors. This is when I try to minimize exposure, be polite, and don't confide!*

SUPPORT SYSTEMS

As wonderful as friends can be, they won't be able to provide all the support and understanding you'll need unless they, too, have Bipolar children. It's extremely important to create a formal support system that can help you deal with all the difficult feelings and emotions that are involved in living with and loving a Bipolar child. There are a variety of formal and informal organizations that can help you get connected with the specific support you need. (See the list in the *Additional Resources* section.)

♥ *I just returned home from my Mothers of Bipolars (also known as the MOB) monthly meeting. This is always an emotionally draining evening for me. I spend much of my time feeling pretty knowledgeable and experienced about being the mother of a Bipolar child. Then I spend a few hours with these amazing women, some of whom have been dealing with this for a decade or more longer than I have. I quickly realize that you can never truly be an expert on something that is constantly changing and that is different for every person.*

I sometimes feel like I have gotten through the darkest days and I'm coming down the home stretch. In reality, I have just begun and, unless I come upon a crystal ball, there is no way to make even an educated guess at what lies ahead. I look into these women's eyes and see emotions so powerful that I literally have to look away because it is so intense. Whether it is pain, fear, desperation, triumph, relief or exhaustion, it is so familiar to me. I feel an intense connection with them. Very few actual words have to be spoken to speak volumes to those who understand your situation.

To look from the outside at this group of people, you would never be able to guess what could have possibly brought us together. We are all different types of women from all different types of lives, sitting and laughing, joking, crying, and talking intensely. If you eavesdropped a little you would not believe what you were hearing: children trying to harm themselves, psychiatric hospitals, medications, husbands, psychiatrists and whatever else may come up that particular evening. It might not look like it from the outside, especially when we're venting our emotions, but this is a group of incredibly strong, capable, caring women. I don't know how I would get through everything I need to survive without these women.

"I've always known that what I had to offer Cindy, as a fellow mom, was in no way unimportant, but it was never quite enough. With two children who easily sailed through every developmental and emotional stage, my perspective was valuable, but not entirely relevant. I did sometimes point out that Julie was doing or experiencing the same things as my son who was the same age and helped Cindy remember that not everything about Julie was

totally Bipolar in nature. There is absolutely no way, though, that a parent without a Bipolar child can completely empathize with everything the parent of a Bipolar child goes through. Fortunately, I had seen Julie at her worst. I had spent countless hours brainstorming with Cindy about how to help her child. I believed that everything Cindy said about what she was dealing with was true. I just couldn't fully comprehend the depth of emotion that both she and Julie experience. When Cindy found a group of other moms of Bipolar children, I knew that she had found the extra support she needed. She often was more stressed out after meetings than before, but she had finally found people who didn't need explanations, who talked reality rather than hopeful wishes. They gave Cindy a reflection on her life that no other friend or family member had been able to do. I listen in awe when she calls me to debrief after these meetings. Cindy needs me to be her friend and support her as a fellow mom and as a woman, but she needs that group to be her support system for dealing with Bipolar Disorder." (Sheryl)

FAMILY SUPPORT

The desire for our parents and family members to see us as successful parents and strong people can make it hard to admit that we need help, to ask for it when we need it, or accept it when it is offered. It can also be hard to accept support from our family members because we want to shield them from the mental health tornado that creates such havoc in our own lives. We also need to have one aspect of our lives that remains unaffected by mental illness. Nevertheless, our families can be a strong, consistent and valuable support system if we let them into the difficult aspects of our lives.

On the flip side, if you are comfortable asking for and receiving help from your parents or other family members, make sure you aren't taking advantage of them. They, too, will get stressed from dealing with your Bipolar child and will need support as they deal with their complicated emotions about what you and your child deal with.

"We were overjoyed that Cindy and Jeff were expecting. We had a special room ready for the new baby at our house because we wanted to be a big part of her life. When Julie was born, we were like most new grandparents with their first grandbaby. She was the center of the universe. We wanted to see her and be with her all the time. We were thrilled at each milestone in her

development. It was evident to us that Julie was the most gifted child who had ever been born. She was so tiny, yet she walked at nine months and talked in sentences soon thereafter. Only another grandparent can imagine how you literally swell with pride just looking at your precious grandchild. When she started attending a gifted school, we were bragging at every opportunity about her amazing abilities.

When Julie stayed at our house overnight or when her parents went on vacation, we had quite a time getting her to sleep. Controlling her behavior was very challenging. But we knew that Cindy and Jeff were feeling overwhelmed, so we really wanted to be supportive. We didn't know what to think of Julie's temperament; maybe it was her 'giftedness' that was making things so hard.

When Julie was three years old, Cindy started going to doctors trying to find some answers. When she told us about Julie's Bipolar diagnosis, we were in shock, just devastated. This little child was the light of our lives. We had just assumed she would do great things in her life. Did this mean that all of our dreams were crushed? For a while we couldn't admit to ourselves that her future might be anything less than amazing. Our hearts were breaking—for Julie, for our daughter, and for Jeff.

At times, taking care of Julie was just too much for us. We wanted to help, but when we tried we often failed. Sometimes Julie would be totally out of control and by the time her parents came home our nerves were completely shot. Despite our efforts to educate ourselves, we still felt like failures in caring for our own granddaughter. Cindy sensed that we were overwhelmed, so she asked for our help less and less often. When we did baby-sit for Julie, we were reluctant to tell Cindy about any problems that occurred. We thought that she already had so much on her plate, we didn't want to add to her burden. We also thought that Cindy didn't want us to relate our difficulties to her—that we should just 'buck up.' Many times we felt as though Cindy was withholding, shutting us out. She now explains that she was trying to protect us from the worst of it. In retrospect, I wish we had been more open with Cindy and that Cindy had been more forthcoming with us.

Having a Bipolar child in the family profoundly affects everyone in the extended family, including aunts, uncles and cousins. As for being a grandparent of a Bipolar child, this is definitely one of life's really big challenges. You probably won't be able to 'fix' this one for your child and, if *you're like us, you will feel guilty and helpless at times. Family dynamics can be pretty complicated. That's why it's so important for all members of the family to be honest and be able to share their feelings candidly. Some of those conversations will be difficult, but it's better than keeping things bottled up or having a strained relationship.*

Now that Julie is 11 years old, we've established the close bond that we always wanted. We spend lots of time with her. She knows beyond a doubt that we are always there for her and that we love her unconditionally. It makes us extremely proud to see how incredibly well she is doing. There are so many good reasons to have high hopes for Julie's future these days."
(Julie's Mimi and Dee)

LIFE BALANCE

You don't constantly have to be doing something productive for your child or your family. Creating fun, relaxation and contentment for yourself is productive, just in an intangible way. But even if you know that having life balance is important, it's rarely easy to figure out how to get it.

The first step to creating life balance is the one most people neglect: defining what it means for you. Does it mean having some time to yourself each day or each week? Does it mean being able to be flexible enough in your schedule to take care of yourself as well as your family? Does it mean feeling happy rather than stressed? Once you know what you want, you can use the following suggestions to help create it. We suggest that you try to do something from each of the following categories on a regular basis, but we also recognize the reality of your busy life. So, pick out the things that are most important to you and try hard to do them as much as possible. Remember, when you take care of yourself, you are modeling positive behavior for your child.

Relaxation/Indulgence:

Try to do something that feels good to you every day. Indulge yourself, even if it's only for five minutes! There are simple things in life that can be quite pleasurable—a piece of chocolate, a cocktail, a nap in the middle of the day, a night out with friends, a foot rub, or a good book can make all the difference in the world. These things can keep you energized and remind you that you are a person, separate from your child and your responsibilities to her. As simple as it sounds, it can be hard to remember in the middle of a stressful, busy day. Schedule the same few minutes each day for some personal relaxation time, put a note on your fridge to remind you to take a few minutes here and there, or do whatever it takes to make yourself slow down for a little while every day.

"I feel so trapped by this disease. There is just never enough of me to go around. I have to work more in order to pay for all the therapy and medication my son needs, but he also needs me at home with him more. No matter what I'm paying attention to, something else is being neglected. It makes me want to scream when people tell me I need to take care of myself, too. Don't they know that if I stop to take care of myself I will pay the price on the other end by suffering with my son's illness even worse! It's such a delicate balancing act. I'm trying to figure out some ways to take care of both of us at the same time. So far, the only thing I've found is the movies. We both get a chance to relax and focus on something outside of ourselves. Maybe some day I'll actually get to take some time to myself." (Monique)

"I get really anxious as I wait in my car to pick up my son. I just know I'm about to let a little tornado in with me. I've found that if I bring a magazine with me and get to school a few minutes early, I can relax and enjoy my last few calm moments for the day. Rather than dreading going to pick him up, I'm more relaxed and have more tolerance. Things actually seem to go better for both of us." (Hannah)

Positive Reinforcement:

Everybody occasionally (or often) needs to hear something nice about themselves. Hopefully, there are people in your life who will give you positive verbal reinforcement about what you're doing without you having to ask for it. Make sure you know whom you can call when you need to get some good, but realistic, feedback.

It's also important to try saying something nice to yourself every day. It feels very strange at first, but it's okay to pat yourself on the back on a regular basis. It seems to be in our parental make-up to criticize ourselves and take the blame for everything that is not perfect about our children. It doesn't feel as natural to validate ourselves and consciously tell ourselves how well we are doing at a very difficult job. No one knows better what we deal with every day than we do. It's wonderful to acknowledge being patient when you wanted to scream, getting almost everything done today, saying just the right thing at just the right time, handling a sticky situation well, or making a good decision. It feels good to be proud of yourself and to recognize and appreciate your accomplishments.

> *"Now that we've had Kate's diagnosis for a few years, I've realized that just when I think I can't cope any more, a calm spell comes along. I've also realized that I actually am functioning rather well. Even when I feel like I just can't go on, I really can. I just have to remind myself that at some point things will get easier."* (Dale)

Acknowledging Negative Feelings:

It's exhausting, frustrating, and depressing to have to constantly be vigilant to protect and care for your child now and to worry about his future safety and happiness. There will be many times when you hate Bipolar Disorder and what it's done to you, your child and your family. Don't beat yourself up for having negative feelings, even if they show up as gallows humor. In many cases, it is easier to laugh than to cry. However they show up, it's better to acknowledge these feelings and try to improve them than to ignore and suppress them. It's also helpful to recognize that these negative feelings are normal, expected, and aren't really directed at your child, so you shouldn't feel guilty about them. They relate to how you feel about the realities of life with Bipolar Disorder. Just make sure that when you vent some of your difficult emotions, you're doing it with people who truly understand that you adore your child, you're just relieving some tension.

> *"I used to be such a happy, optimistic person. That person is long gone. I feel so defeated. I hate this disease."* (Selena)

> *"I feel like Emily sucks the energy right out of me. I am so drained that I can't imagine having to do this for another day, let alone years and years."* (Cathy)

> ♥   *I occasionally throw myself a "pity party." No one else is invited but me and I spend some time really feeling sorry for myself. I may spend a*

couple of hours while my kids are in school watching the most mindless television talk shows I can find, or I may just lay in bed and cry. I don't answer the phone or talk to anyone (but myself). For some reason, and I don't really care why, I feel so much better when I'm done and usually I'm ready to face life again by the time the kids get home from school.

Pure and Simple Fun:

It's not enough just to survive all this. You also deserve to have some fun, too. It's great if some of that fun can be with your child, but the reality is that every parent needs time away from the kids. There's nothing wrong with wanting to get away a bit. Even doctors and nurses who work in psychiatric hospitals take breaks and they only work 8-12 hours at a time!

Figure out what is fun for you and how much time and resources you have to create it. Maybe you can't go to a spa, but you can have a manicure once in a while. Maybe you and your partner can't get away for a weekend, but a date night is better than nothing. Maybe you can't have a long vacation, but you can take a long weekend away. Maybe fun is sitting down in your house when no one else is home and reading a good book or doing a jigsaw puzzle. Whatever it may be and for however long you can manage it, try not to go through life without simple enjoyment. It will make you a better parent for having had it.

PROFESSIONAL SUPPORT

As wonderful as our friends, family, and support groups are, they may not be able to provide all the support the parent of a Bipolar child requires. You probably have a lot of scary thoughts, intense emotions and complicated choices that may not be appropriate to discuss with anyone but a professional. The stress in your life is significant enough that you run a real risk of developing psychological problems that need to be addressed by an expert. As one mom wrote on an Internet chartroom, "having a BP child is certainly not conducive towards mental health for anyone."

Don't wait until you're in crisis. Professional mental healthcare is probably something you're going to need, and even want, on a regular basis. Having it can help you avoid your own crises, not to mention help you cope better on a day-to-day basis. Your therapist can be the one person in your life who is totally focused on taking care of your needs and feelings. If he isn't, switch therapists! Finding a good therapist who can help you deal with your life as the parent of a Bipolar child is almost as important as having a good therapist for your child.

MEDICATION SUPPORT

Just as your child may not be able to control his feelings and thoughts without chemical assistance, you may not either. Just as it's okay for your child to be taking medication that he needs, it's okay for you to need it, too. Friends, relaxation, support groups and therapy just might not be enough to keep you feeling sufficiently stable to handle all your responsibilities and still feel good about yourself. If you're finding that your own negative thoughts, lack of energy, dulled emotions, anxiety, fluctuating moods and/or sense of hopelessness are getting in the way of your ability to function, it's time to talk to your own doctor about medication.

"Once I started on Zoloft, I had a whole new perspective on life. Suddenly things didn't seem quite so dismal and overwhelming. It didn't change any of the circumstances of my life, but it did make them feel slightly more manageable. I feel better about myself and my ability to cope with my son than I have in a long time." (Hailey)

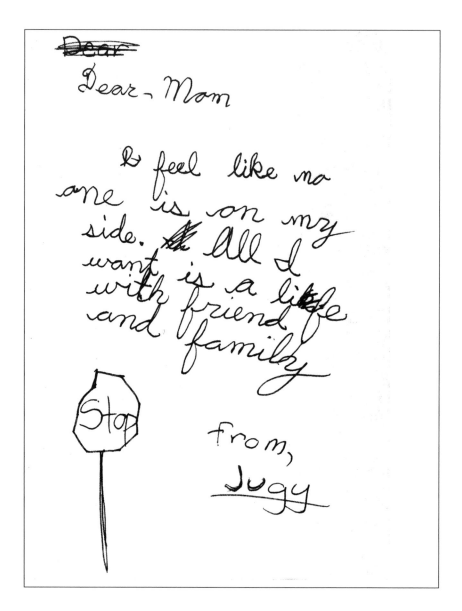

A note from Julie, 9 years old

SECTION SIX:

Helping Your Child Live with Bipolar Disorder

14
The Reality of Your Child's Daily Life

Just as your daily routine is different from that of parents whose children do not have Bipolar Disorder, your Bipolar child's day is different, too. She faces challenges and frustrations throughout her day just as you do. The better you understand what she's dealing with, the better you can support her. Knowing what she deals with may also help you separate her behavior from her intent so you can be frustrated with the situation, but not with her.

The stories in this chapter, some from parents and many directly from the mouths of children with Bipolar Disorder, will help you gain an understanding of what your child may experience throughout a typical day. The "things to try" suggestions will help you and your child deal with the situations these kids face. These ideas aren't intended to be foolproof solutions, but rather things to try as you consciously experiment to figure out what works best for your child's particular needs and moods.

"Hi, my name is Julie. I am 8 years old and I have Bipolar Disorder. I think it is really hard because I have to take a lot of medicines and go to a lot of doctors' appointments. I really need a lot of help. I know that some of you kids out there might need help too. Sometimes I get really mad and I can't

figure out what to do, but I know people still love me. Some advice for other kids with Bipolar—I think you should just relax and do your job. I know it's hard but your job is to learn as much as you can about your feelings so that you can control them better."

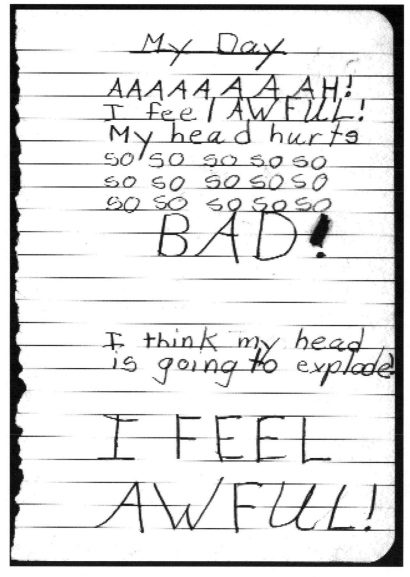

An entry from 10 year-old Julie's diary.

A DAY IN THE LIFE OF A BIPOLAR CHILD

Following are common challenges that Bipolar kids and their parents face throughout the day and suggestions of how you can help make your child's life easier.

Waking up:

> *"When I wake in the morning I'm so dizzy it's hard to get up. I feel so tired and drowsy in the morning I can't even open my eyes."* (Julie, 10)

> *"The part of the day I dread the most is the morning when I have to get 8 year-old Jeremy out of bed. The house goes from totally peaceful to complete chaos in a matter of seconds. It could be quiet and calm then when he wakes up it is screaming, yelling, fighting, and crying."* (Maya)

Things to try: Set an alarm clock for earlier in the morning so your child can hit the snooze button a couple of times before getting up. If your child is on medication, wake her up early, give her meds and let her sleep a little longer. Offer highly motivating rewards for getting up on time. Change your expectations and accept that this is an unpleasant part of the day.

Morning activities: Getting dressed, brushing teeth, straightening room, eating breakfast, getting school stuff ready

> *"My family teases me about taking so long to get ready each morning. It's just so hard to think about all the clothes in my closet and drawers. I can't decide what to wear. All the choices swirl around in my head and I end up sitting on my bed staring at my closet until my mom comes to help me."* (Denise, 8)

> *"Every morning, the first thing on my mind is being dead. I look at myself in the mirror and tell myself that killing myself is not an option today. Sometimes I even tell myself 'stop!'"* (Jesse, 10)

Things to try: Get everything ready the night before. Pack up the backpack and lay out clothes. Let your child go to sleep in the clothes he will wear the next day. Have a morning checklist for your child to follow so you do not have to constantly tell him what to do. Give rewards for accomplishing even basic tasks independently. Decide and focus on what is really important. Give your child choices of chores that can be done after school or at a more productive, less stressful time. Give your child permission to be as grumpy as he wants as long as he is getting ready. Accept and expect that you will have to be more involved in getting your child ready than most other parents.

Taking medications:

"I hate being called to the nurse's office every day before lunch to take my medicine. I try to look really busy at that time so maybe the teacher will forget to send me. I always end up last in the lunch line and I'm sick of all the kids asking me why I have to always go to the nurse." (Julie, 7)

"I get so embarrassed when my friends see me taking medicine. I am so afraid that they will make fun of me or think I am sick or weird." (Monica, 11)

Things to try: Give a reward after your child takes her medicine without a fuss. Explain in a positive way why she needs to take her meds. Tell her it helps her be the "boss of her mad" or helps her to be happier or less afraid, etc. Never give in to her not wanting to take meds. Ask the doctor about different forms that may work better, such as sustained release (less frequent doses), liquid versus pills, or vice versa. Give your child language to respond to others asking why she takes medicine. Depending on what your child is comfortable with and her age, this can be anything from, "they are special vitamins" to "N.O.Y.B." (none of your business), to, "they help me feel better" to "my mom makes me" to a detailed lecture on brain chemistry. Talk with your child to see what feels right, but preparing her in advance is critical.

School:

"I used to be really smart. Now, it seems like everything is so much easier for all the other kids. I think I am the dumbest one in the class." (Julie, 11)

"I count down the minutes until school's over and my mom picks me up, then I don't have to try so hard to be good. It makes me so tired to try and be good all day long. I just want to go home so I can let my mad and my sillies out." (Joel, 9)

Things to try: Visit an educational psychologist or therapist who specializes in identifying the best type of learning environment for special needs kids. Research school issues such as using an Individual Education Plan (IEP), special education classes, private schools that address learning disorders, and non-traditional school options to help you identify the best school options for your child. Change schools if necessary in order to obtain the type of assistance that meets your child's particular needs. Keep copies of all test and evaluation results so you can share them with new teachers. Have your child take IQ and psycho-educational tests on a regular basis so you can identify and address changes in abilities as soon as possible.

Stay in regular contact with teachers and administrators to share information on your child's progress and what is and isn't working for her at any particular time. Recognize that the teacher has the right and responsibility to set and enforce behavior expectations at school. Supporting the teacher lets your child experience another adult's rules and guidance. If you and the teacher are working together and staying in communication, it also prevents your child from manipulating the situation to pit you against each other.

Don't expect your child to be good at everything. Communicate with educators about what she is and isn't good at. Talk with the parents of other students in the class to get their perspectives on the workload, teaching style and class dynamics so you can make more informed decisions. Sometimes there might be general problems, not just problems that your child is experiencing because of Bipolar Disorder. Remember to praise her for what she does well in addition to coaching her to do better in other areas.

Ask the school to make some accommodations, such as:

▲ Seat the child near the teacher—up front or within a 5-foot radius of where the teacher usually stands or sits

▲ Eliminate timed tests whenever possible

▲ Eliminate unnecessary copying or tedious written work and allow extra time for written assignments

▲ Control the amount of written work so that the completion time is similar to that of most students even though the quantity is less, but be careful to keep quality and expectations high

"Carrie does really well in school—when she wants to. Being well rounded isn't everything. She's so into science that I'm sure she'll discover great things. So what if she won't be able to spell, doesn't know when the Civil War took place, and has no concept of what geometry is about!" (Nora)

"Jordan and Julie were together from the time they were three and in preschool through first grade at a private school for the gifted. Cindy and I shared a lot of notes on how our children were doing with the teachers, their homework, their behavior in school, and their attitudes toward school. Several times I had to confirm to teachers that what Cindy was saying about Julie's behavior and struggles at home were real. The teachers just didn't believe it since, according to them and to Jordan, Julie's behavior in school was fairly normal at that point. In fact, she clearly was extremely gifted.

In third grade, Julie's giftedness not only seemed less apparent but it seemed like she was experiencing some learning disabilities. Poor Cindy had to go from one extreme to another in dealing with teachers and educational issues. Yet again she had to try to decipher whether Julie's problems were part of the Bipolar Disorder or something else going on. Poor Julie was convinced that she had gone from being smart to being stupid. Yet another aspect of her life was being dramatically affected by her psychodevelopmental disorder.

Cindy and I went from sharing almost every aspect of our children's educational experiences to talking fairly superficially about it. I didn't want to hurt her feelings by talking about how well my kids were doing. She didn't want me to feel like I should hold back, and I knew she was still interested in my kids' progress, but our conversations just weren't the same anymore. How could they be? Our issues and experiences were at completely different ends of the spectrum. Still, we started to talk more about strategies for dealing with the school system in general than about our kids' specific performances and found that our conversations were helpful for both of us again." (Sheryl)

Homework:

> *" I feel upset and mad when I'm doing my homework because I have so much. I'm scared to do it because I have a really hard time with math. I know I'm going to fail because I'm so bad at math."* (Julie, 10)

> *"I get so overwhelmed with everything that needs to get done that I can't get myself to start on anything. If I can get myself to start on something, the thoughts about everything else that I have to do keep running through my head so I can't concentrate on what I'm doing."* (Mark, 8)

> *"Studying for a test is easy if it's something that I like. If it isn't, I don't see why I should do it. The teacher is just making me do something stupid. I don't like being told what to do."* (Kyle, 11)

Things to try: Experiment to find the best time for homework. Your child may need playtime or physical activity first or may do better doing it right when he gets home. Allow your child to do homework when he has the most energy, which might be at nine o'clock at night. Establish a definite daily homework routine at a consistent time in a consistent place—four times per week. If there is no homework, use the time for reading. Your child is likely feeling overwhelmed. Break down assignments into smaller pieces. Cover up all problems except the one he is working on. Make a prioritized list of everything that needs to be done. Put away all other homework except what he is currently working on. Make a schedule or checklist so he can cross things off when he's done them. Hire a tutor, possibly a college student or a teacher with extra time, so homework is one less thing you are battling over—he may do much better with someone outside the family. Elicit the school's help—modifications may need to be made.

Ask your child's teacher for help with the following strategies:

▲ Have an agreement that enables you to modify or shorten homework assignments when your child seems overwhelmed or at his limit or is just not doing well in general

▲ Provide very clear written assignments

▲ Make a prioritized list of homework to be done

▲ Break large or long-term assignments into parts with due dates

▲ Provide examples of desired performance

▲ Occasionally allow the child to dictate answers and have someone else do the writing

▲ Encourage keyboarding skills and minimize the act of handwriting

Extracurricular activities:

"Sometimes I just start crying during baseball practice. I don't even know why. My mom told me just to say that I'm really sad and I don't know why, but I'll be okay." (John, 6)

"Samantha couldn't handle team sports at all. She couldn't seem to get ready on time. She couldn't pay attention when the coach was talking to the team. She got frustrated waiting her turn. It ended up being more struggle than it was worth. She wasn't getting any pleasure out of it and the rest of the family was stressed every time there was a practice or game." (Sandy)

Things to try: Make sure your child really wants to do the activity. It's a huge commitment and has to be something she really wants. Be realistic about your child's abilities—it may be that just daily living, school and family are all your child can handle. Extracurricular activities are optional!! Don't feel like they have to be a part of your child's life just because all the other kids are doing them. If you do decide to get involved in extracurricular activities, individual sports might be a better option than team sports so your child doesn't have to concentrate on the social stuff. Volunteer to help so you can supervise and see how your child is doing. Maybe an at-home hobby would be better. Another option is to schedule activities for your child's best times of day. Make sure that your child doesn't have to make a quick transition from one activity to another—shifting their attention from one thing to another can be difficult for Bipolar children.

Doctor appointments:

"After school, all the other kids get to play outside or go to soccer practice. I have to go to dumb doctor appointments." (Shelby, 7)

"That stupid idiot had to poke me two times in each arm to take my blood. I hate her!" (Julie, 8)

"All we do is sit in her dumb office and talk. She has dragon eyes and she wants to talk about stuff that's really hard. This isn't helping me. I don't know why I have to do this. My medicine makes me better, why does my mom make me go there?" (Justin, 10)

Things to try: Schedule appointments at a time of day that tends to be a less stressful time for your child. Create a "going to the doctor routine" that includes fun activities or treats before and after the appointment. This could include stopping at a convenience store where she can choose any candy she wants, renting a movie, or stopping at the arcade. If your child acts up before or during the doctor appointment, don't do the fun part of the routine that comes after the appointment. Never, never cancel a doctor's appointment because of your child's poor behavior—it's actually good for the doctor to see your child at her worst. Also, if you give in once and cancel an appointment, your child will never stop trying to get you to do it again. If appropriate, during difficult times during the appointment (such as while blood is being drawn), distract your child by talking with her about the fun activity you're going to do after the appointment. Allow your child as much control over the appointment as possible. Ask if she wants to have her blood drawn first or last, for example. Have a stash of small toys that you bring with you and let her pick what to hold or play with during the exam. Encourage her to keep a list of the questions she wants to ask the doctor about her body, her moods, and her medicines. Encourage her to talk directly with the doctor instead of having you talk for her.

Being with friends:

"I have no friends. Everyone hates me. Everyone always gets mad at me. Friends are stupid!" (Jack, 11)

"I hate Sara. She left and said she never wanted to play with me again. I punched her and pushed her off the bed when she wouldn't play the game I wanted to play. Her game was just plain dumb, no one would want to play that. And now I am grounded for no reason at all. She should be the one in trouble for not being nice to me." (Courtney, 10)

"I do whatever it takes to get what I want. I know exactly what to say to get my way. Sometimes I just make my friends upset because it's fun. I like to see what I can get them to do. My mom says I should stop being so manipulative, but I can't help it." (Bryan, 12)

Things to try: If your child is young enough that you have some control over who his friends are, choose them carefully. If your child is old enough to choose his own friends, think about which friendships to encourage more than others. It's better to have a few good friends than lots of friends who cause more stress for you or your child. Invite certain friends over for certain types of activities. For example, some friends might be better than others to take to the pool or have for a sleepover. Some might do well on their own while others should only be invited if their parent stays, too. Carefully control how many friends are over at once. One or two is probably best. Plan some activities your child can do with the friend(s) so he has options from which to choose. Otherwise, negotiating with the friend about what activities to do could get overwhelming. Have friends over to your house rather than having your child go to theirs. Supervise play dates. Be ready to step in to redirect the kids if they start having trouble. Encourage more structured activities (such as a board game, a movie, or a trip to an arcade or fun restaurant) or less structured activities (such as a visit to a playground, or riding bikes) depending on what seems appropriate. After the play date, discuss with your child what went well and what didn't and how he might handle difficult situations better next time. Set a code that your child can use to tell you that he's ready for the friend to go home without having to say so in front of the friend. Make sure the friend's parent is home so you can take him home if your child's behavior gets out of hand or is about to. Remember that you don't need to tell all the friends' parents about your child's Bipolar Disorder. Only do so if it seems necessary and helpful.

♥ *Parents always want the best playmates for their children. It is even more important with children like Julie. Unfortunately, she seems to be drawn to friends she can manipulate and control. She also likes friends who are extremely forgiving, too forgiving. We always think about protecting our own children, but I also must always do my best to protect the children with whom Julie comes in contact. This illness is not their burden to carry, and Julie's behavior can be very disturbing and scary to them. Even at eight years old, I still feel like I have to closely supervise her playtimes with other children. I have learned to see the early signs of a play date going downhill. Sometimes I can redirect her and sometimes I can't.*

There are many other things I try to keep in mind. Older children seem to be better choices, they tend to be more mature and handle tough social situations more easily. Parents of older children seem to be more relaxed and understanding of other children's not-so-perfect behavior as well. People with only younger children don't know from experience what is normal childhood behavior for a particular age. They only have the image of how they want their children to be, which we all know is never quite on the mark.

There are certain parents that I have learned to trust, respect and communicate with. I feel comfortable letting her play at a home where I know that the adult will be kind to her and to me if the play date does not go well. I also try to have Julie play with her friends at our house as much as possible. This gives me much more control over Julie's behavior and keeps her protected from not having me there to help her if she starts to spiral out of control.

I know my friends have struggled to try and love, understand, and be patient with Julie, while simultaneously protecting their own children from Julie's behaviors. This has been very painful for me. It is devastating to realize how damaging my little girl can actually be. As I'm sure you can imagine, being friends with me and Julie is not the easiest thing in the world.

"I like it when Maria, 8, plays with kids who are not the oldest child in their families. Parents tend to have high expectations of oldest kids. Once parents are dealing with their younger kids, they are more relaxed and accepting of the wide range of normal in kids' behavior. This makes it easier for them to understand when Maria isn't perfect." (Sherrie)

Nighttime:

> *"It is so hard to fall asleep when there are 500 thoughts running through my mind. It's too much to listen to and I can't relax and fall asleep." (Joseph, 8)*

> *"Everyone else is asleep and I feel alone and scared." (Julie, 10)*

Things to try: Keep a constant but non-irritating noise (such as a CD, recorded white noise, or a video) going to minimize other noises that might startle your child. Expect your child to stay in her room even if she's not in bed and preferably in her bed even if she's having trouble falling asleep. Keep books or toys right next to the bed for your child to play with in bed when she can't sleep, put a TV with a remote control in your child's room, lock areas of the house that you do not want your child to enter during the night, put an alarm on the outside doors so if your child tries to go outside you'll know, and/or use a baby monitor to listen to what is going on in your child's room.

> ♥ *I was desperate to get Julie to stay in her bed long enough to actually have the possibility of falling asleep. I finally ignored all my preconceived judgments about having a TV in a child's room, and installed a small TV/VCR combo in her room. It isn't hooked up to cable, so she can only watch movies. At least I still have some sense of control over what she's watching in there. It actually really helped and it also gives her something quiet and relaxing to do when she can't sleep in the middle of the night. Once again, I found myself doing something I never thought I would do and reminding myself that all my old rules don't apply.*

CREATING STRUCTURE FOR YOUR CHILD

Of course, just when something starts to work in one situation, that situation will probably change somewhat. The challenge is to continually make incremental changes to try to find what works and what doesn't while keeping the key elements of what works as consistent as possible. You might feel like you're constantly tweaking everything you do, but that's going to be a regular part of dealing with your child's daily struggles.

The parents of non-Bipolar children can make an exception to the rules or routine once in a while. You can't. They can explain to their child why that certain situation is somewhat different and therefore justifies a change in the routine, and then go back to normal the next time. Their children might fuss a little, but will probably get back into the swing of things fairly easily. Your child on the other hand, will never let you forget it if you bend the rules, let alone break them, even once. You will have set a new precedent. Your child will rage and rage until you give in again. After all, it worked once—it might work again! Therefore, keep things as consistent as possible. The more your child knows what to expect, knows the limits of what she can and can't change, and understands what she can and can't control, the more calm the day is likely to be for both of you.

On the other hand, while there are many differences between dealing with your child and dealing with a child who doesn't have Bipolar Disorder, there are also many similarities. Make sure you are reading books on general childhood development and sharing parenting stories with parents of non-Bipolar children. Some of the behavior challenges you'll face will just be the normal, developmental, social and intellectual, age-appropriate fluctuations that all kids experience. It's helpful to know the difference between Bipolar symptoms and normal difficult behavior when you're trying to help your child through them.

15
Handling the Rough Times

Julie's 3rd grade art teacher loved this picture. It hung on the wall in the school for over a month. She didn't notice that the person on the top of the building is saying, "I'm committing suicide" and that there is a dead body lying on the street below.

COPING IN UNUSUALLY DIFFICULT SITUATIONS

Most kids, and therefore most parents, have rough times as they enter a difficult developmental stage, face a major life transition, or just have a particularly moody phase. As the parent of a Bipolar child, you, too, will have those difficult times, as well as the everyday challenges involved with Bipolar Disorder. Then there will be the times that are way beyond your normal level of difficulty—times when your child's behavior and/or emotional problems become significantly worse or substantially prolonged.

When you're faced with a very rough time, whether it's a specific incident or a particularly stressful phase, it's difficult, but important, not to get caught up in the storm. Keep it about your child, not you. If you let your own feelings escalate along with your child's, both of you will have a hard time calming down. Instead, try to identify the signals of a situation that is just so bad that there's nothing you can do, other than make sure your child is safe. When you're in the middle of such a situation, reassure yourself that you've done the best that you can do, even if that meant doing nothing. Of course, this is easier said than done. It's hard not to feel guilty for letting your child deal with such obviously horrendous feelings on his own.

Next, mentally separate yourself from the problem. Try and remember that your child's behavior is probably very different from his intent. He's not trying to upset you; he's just having such difficult feelings that he can't control himself. And, since the problem is in his brain chemistry, there really isn't anything you can do to make him feel better, other than to assure your child that you are there for him, that you love him, and that you understand that he doesn't mean to be a problem. Try to keep calm, cool and collected so you can protect your child, protect yourself, and remember enough about the situation to describe it in your child's behavior log and communicate it to the therapist and psychiatrist.

Even if you can keep from feeling caught up in your child's rages and misbehaviors, it's still hard not to have negative feelings. Every parent has times when the difficulties of being a parent make them think, "Why did I even have a child," or, "What did I do to deserve this," or, "I wish this kid would just take care of herself or go away so I could get some peace and quiet." These types of feelings are perfectly normal; you may just experience them more frequently than parents whose children don't have a psychodevelopmental disorder. Remember, when these negative feelings pop up, it's better to try to acknowledge and address them than to feel guilty and suppress them. You have every right to be angry, upset, or resentful sometimes. It doesn't mean that you don't love your child. As we've said before, once you've overcome your guilt about having these types of feelings, you can start to work on overcoming them and trying to prevent them from happening as often.

♥ *Julie would often lose control when we were driving. Sometimes I felt like a prisoner, trapped in my own car. When things escalated, I would usually just ignore her, pretend that I couldn't hear her, but every word felt like a physical blow to my heart. It would usually start with something insignificant like what we were having for dinner or her hair getting static cling. Everything was always my fault. She would tell me what a terrible mother I was. She would talk about going to live somewhere else or running away. She would say she knew that I didn't love her and that I never did anything for her. It was a relentless verbal attack that would last the entire duration of the ride.*

On one particularly memorable occasion, there was one of the most beautiful sunsets I think I've ever seen. Brilliant orange and pink clouds cast an incredible glow across the landscape. I was driving home from I don't know where and Julie began a tantrum in the car. Quickly losing control, she was screaming and screaming, louder and louder, longer and longer. It was so intense and so awful I felt as if I might go mad. No matter what I said I could not seem to make a difference. She was chanting, "I hate you! I hate you!" over and over again.

Finally, I pulled over to the side of the road, grabbed my cell phone and got out of the car. My heart was pounding and I began to cry. Julie, in the meantime, was trying to kick out the car window with both of her feet and spitting on the inside of the window, screaming the whole time. I dialed a good friend and said, "If you don't talk me through this, I'm going to kill her!" Needless to say, she talked to me until I pulled myself together. I got back into the car, drove home, and wondered what was happening to my little girl. Shortly after we arrived home, Julie felt great and went about her evening as if nothing had happened. I felt exhausted, depressed, and confused as if I had been hit by a truck. It was almost impossible to believe this was a 6 year-old child.

MAKING DIFFICULT DECISIONS

If your child is experiencing rough times that are more intense, longer-lasting and/or more frequent than normal, you have to decide whether or not some additional or different action needs to be taken from a treatment standpoint and from a parenting perspective. Unfortunately, there are so many inter-related factors when you're dealing with Bipolar Disorder that it's often difficult to find one solution that will handle all the various aspects of a situation. It's also easy to get so caught up in the forest that you forget to see the trees. When you start to feel overwhelmed or incapable of identifying the optimal solution, try mentally stepping back from the situation. Identify, if you can, what seems to be the most significant, critical, or life-affecting aspect of the problem. Identify your options for dealing with that. Then, evaluate how well each option will address all the other sub-problems. It might even help to write down the pros and cons of each option. You might not be able to find one all-encompassing solution, but approaching the situation strategically can help you make the best choice.

Once you've made a choice, of course, it's natural to wonder whether a different choice would have been somewhat better or, when things don't work out as well as you had hoped, to think you made a totally wrong decision. We all have these doubts. Even parents whose children don't have Bipolar Disorder go through this. Their decisions just tend not to involve things like medication that can cause life-long side effects. When parents of Bipolar kids feel like we've messed up, the consequences to our children can seem enormous.

When you find yourself second-guessing your decision, think back to what was going on at the time you made it. What information did you have then? What were the most significant problems? What were the options available at the time? What were the experts recommending? Now that you know more or have seen the consequences of your decision, it might seem like you made a bad choice, but you probably made the best decision you could have made, given the information you had at the time. If you've gotten this far in this book, you aren't the type of parent who is making impulsive decisions or consciously choosing options that aren't best for your child. As the saying goes, "hindsight is always 20/20." Just take the information and experience you have gained and try to apply it the next time you and your child encounter a rough time. The situation and choices may be totally different then, but the process you need to go through to make the best possible choice probably won't be.

"Ashley's condition all of a sudden deteriorated a lot. After almost a year of what, from our perspective, was relative stability, she became so out of control so fast that something had to be done quickly. She had just had her med levels adjusted because she'd had a huge growth spurt, she was about to take her final tests of the year, we had a big family vacation planned in two weeks and my husband was out of the country on a business trip. I was frantic. Should I immediately hospitalize her, wait for an appointment with the pediatrician and the psychiatrist to discuss changing her med levels again, keep her home from school regardless of her grades, or assume that school stress was too much and meet with her teacher yet again about giving Ashley more time on tests? Should I assume that she was going to have to have intense regular therapy so I should cancel the vacation that was non-refundable if cancelled with less than 14 days notice? I clearly had to do something fast and of course, it was the weekend, so the psychiatrist's partner was on call. My husband was unreachable. I was concerned about taking her to the emergency room because she wasn't acting so out of control or suicidal in a way that anyone else would recognize. I decided that first and foremost, I had to have a professional who understood her and Bipolar Disorder see her. I convinced the doctor on call to contact my regular doctor, who was willing to set up an appointment first thing Monday morning. I left a message at the school and told them that she wouldn't be in on Monday and asked if we could schedule a make-up test. I called the resort to see if they would give me some leeway on the cancellation policy. I cancelled all our weekend plans, set up play dates for my other kids, got potential baby-sitters ready for the other kids in case I needed to take Ashley to the hospital on short notice, then spent the whole weekend with Ashley. I literally didn't leave her alone for a minute. When we went to the doctor appointment, he recommended immediate hospitalization. I feel somewhat guilty that I didn't do that right away. I feel like I wasted valuable treatment time. He reassured me, though, that I didn't do her any harm since I made sure she didn't harm herself. He also agreed that the emergency room staff might not have been knowledgeable enough to deal with her properly at the time. I confirmed the travel arrangements for my husband and other kids and decided that if Ashley and I can go, we will. If we can't, I'll try to talk the resort into a refund since the cancellation is due to medical reasons, but I just can't deal with that right now." (Leslie)

DEALING WITH THE WORST TIME—THE RISK OF SUICIDE

Now that you've learned so much about Bipolar Disorder and are actively getting treatment, you might be tempted not to read this part. After all, good treatment and knowledge can prevent crisis, right? Maybe. Even with the best care, Bipolar Disorder can cause rapid, unexpected and serious problems. The more you know about what could happen, the better prepared you'll be to recognize the situation and quickly and appropriately deal with it. So read on. It won't be easy, but one day you might be glad you got through this information.

Many Bipolar children have episodes when they do physical harm to themselves on purpose. It often happens when they're raging. It's also common for our kids to have grandiose feelings that make them think they are capable of doing extraordinary, often dangerous things without getting hurt. So, even if your child isn't suicidal, her actions may be dangerous. This can make it difficult to determine when these behaviors are merely symptoms of Bipolar Disorder and when they are signs of suicidal tendencies.

Unfortunately, studies about signs of suicidal feelings, suicide statistics, and suicide prevention in people with Bipolar Disorder tend to focus on teens and adults. While suicide attempts and completions are much, much more common in teens and adults, they can and do happen in children. We just don't know the actual statistics on how often.

It's tempting to think that your child is just trying to make you upset by talking about hurting herself, but you can't take that chance. If your child talks about death or suicide, seems preoccupied with danger, and/or behaves in ways that are extremely risky, these could be signs that your child is suicidal. Take them seriously. Don't discount it just because you think she's too young to actually do it.

Since young children are usually under an adult's direct supervision, they are somewhat protected from a serious suicide attempt, but not completely. Your child's youth may actually work against her because she may not be old enough to understand that death is permanent. Suicide might be something that she decides to try because she doesn't know any other way to cope with difficult feelings or an uncomfortable situation. A child is capable of purposefully exposing herself to dangers that could kill her. A 6 year-old can and has climbed to the roof of a house and jumped. A 10 year-old can wander off and put himself in danger. These types of attempts should be taken just as seriously as attempts by adults who take too many pills or shoot themselves. If you don't provide extra treatment when your child seriously threatens or actually makes a suicide attempt, she may have a completed attempt sooner or later. So, if you think, even just once, that this could be what's going on, ACT! Don't leave your child unattended without a responsible adult watching over her. Keep her in the safest place possible. Try to get her to talk about her feelings and frustrations. Help her think of more positive ways to deal with them.

Also, talk to a mental health professional, preferably one who is on her healthcare team. If you can't get your child in to see the psychiatrist, who should be your first contact, at least try to talk with the psychiatrist on the phone to see if he/she thinks your child needs to go to the emergency room of a regular hospital or a psychiatric hospital. The doctor might suggest taking your child to a non-hospital treatment program. He/she might suggest changing a medication level and coming in for a session soon. It's when you can't talk to the psychiatrist for professional advice that the going gets extremely rough. You just have to decide what to do. Doing nothing until you get professional advice is not an option. Talk to the therapist if you can get hold of him/her. Call a suicide prevention hotline for help. If you feel your child is in imminent danger, call 911 or take her to an emergency room. Even if the action you take isn't the optimal solution, doing something is better than doing nothing. It is better to overreact that under-react. Getting some help is better than dealing with it alone.

♥   *The idea of a child taking her life or injuring herself is one of the most terrifying thoughts a parent can imagine. The first time Julie talked about killing herself she was 5 years old. How does a 5 year-old even think of something like that? She was having a tantrum—crying, kicking, screaming, writhing around, and throwing things. She started yelling down the stairs to me that no one loved her, that she hated herself, that we'd all be better off if she killed herself and wasn't around anymore. That was the beginning. She started threatening to jump out her window or run away forever. One time she hung over the stair railing (about a 12-foot fall) and just screamed, "I'm going to drop, I'm going to drop!" She was literally hanging by just her fingertips.*

"Anneka sometimes feels that she's stupid and that she can't do anything right. She hates everything about her life and often talks about not wanting

to be around anymore. She says things like, 'If I jump out the window no one would miss me and you would all be happy that I am gone,' and 'I am going to get a knife out of the kitchen and cut my head off.' How is a mother supposed to respond to this from a seven year-old child?" (Erika)

"My friends' kids will say things like, 'you hate me and I wish I'd never been born' or, 'I wish I was in a different family.' My child has said, 'I'm going to jump in front of the subway train and make myself dead so I don't have to be with you anymore.'" (Wendi)

HOSPITALIZATION

It's horrible to think of having to put your child into a psychiatric hospital. Visions of *One Flew Over the Cuckoo's Nest*, the girl in the movie *Don't Say a Word* sing-songing, "I'll never teeellll" to Michael Douglas, *Girl, Interrupted* and other Hollywood versions of the loony bin will run through your head. Hospitalization may become necessary, though, if your child is suicidal or homicidal, having a psychotic episode (usually characterized by hallucinations, delusions and a loss of contact with reality), a prolonged period of severe depression, or other symptoms that indicate that her brain chemistry is so out of whack that she requires constant monitoring, a thorough assessment of her round-the-clock behaviors, numerous medical tests to check her medication levels, and/or frequent adjustments to her medication.

The good news is that pediatric mental health wards tend to be very different than the horror stories we see in the movies and our nightmares. Most pediatric psychiatric facilities are more like dorms than like torture chambers. While there are locks on the doors, extensive rules, and almost constant supervision, these strict safety measures are there to protect your child. In a good program, your child will be with children of approximately the same age and functional level, able to participate in the facility's school and age-appropriate activities, able to earn age-appropriate privileges (such as buying candy, getting to walk around outside, or going out to dinner with you) for maintaining safe and appropriate behavior, and be seen frequently by trained therapists. If possible with your insurance, financial and logistical constraints, visit various facilities in your area to find out which one you think is best, just in case you need it in the future and can have a choice in which facility is selected. It can also be very reassuring to know that if you do have to hospitalize your child, there are places that are friendly, caring and specially designed to make things as normal as possible for the patients.

Even when you've accepted the need to hospitalize your child and have found a place that is appropriate, finding the right place with an available bed and getting your insurance to cover it can be next to impossible. Make sure you know the procedures for getting admitted before you need to admit your child. If it is an obvious emergency, such as an attempted suicide, and your child is admitted through an emergency room, you probably won't have much trouble. You will want to try to go to a hospital that is on your insurance plan, to notify the insurance company as soon as possible, and obtain any necessary authorizations for treatment. Hopefully, the emergency room staff and the psychiatric facility's staff will help with or even handle this process. Even if you do everything right, though, it might take the insurance company a long time to approve an inpatient admission that is not done on an emergency basis. Try to have the presence of mind to confirm that the hospital or program knows and is using the right procedures to get the right kind of authorization from the right department of your insurance company for the right type of treatment. Remind them to take notes and get names and phone numbers from insurance company representatives.

"We couldn't find a hospital that has beds for voluntary hospitalization of 8 year-olds. We finally had to call the police to have our daughter transported to an emergency room for evaluation. We could only get her into a hospital when the situation had gotten so bad it really was an emergency. It sure would have been nice to have been able to get her some treatment before things got that bad." (Tanya)

"After Klaire ran out into a busy street on purpose, got so violent we called the police, and had a trip to the emergency room after she put her hand through a window, our insurance company still refused to cover inpatient or partial hospitalization. They said she still didn't meet all the criteria. I think they want her to really hurt herself before they'll do anything." (Morgan)

"The psychiatrist told us that if we consistently saw the violent behavior and threats to run away we had observed the previous night that we needed to take Caley to the hospital. Caley didn't even wait until we left the doctor's

office before she lost it. She screamed that she would not get into the car with us. I forced her into the car, but she continued to scream and repeatedly kicked the seats. As I drove, she opened the door and acted like she was going to jump out. I dropped the cell phone that I had been holding in order to call the psychiatrist, grabbed her by her jacket, and slammed on the brakes. I convinced her to shut the door, but she did it again a few minutes later. I managed to divert her by offering to take her somewhere other than home. I was terrified, so I drove toward the police station that is close to home. She thought I was taking her home, so she went totally ballistic. Thankfully, the police were really helpful. One officer talked with her a lot and told her about all the kids that get hurt when they run away from home. Caley couldn't have cared less. She just kept screaming that she was 'leaving.' The nice policeman offered to escort us to the hospital. In the ER, Caley threw herself against walls, broke furniture and screamed for something to eat, but she wouldn't stop screaming long enough to eat it. The ER staff was amazed at her behavior. Even though they mentioned several times that they had never admitted an 8 year-old before, they did finally admit her." (Annie)

"The only place we could get Crystal into is hours away. It took several days, what seemed like hundreds of phone calls, and repeated explanations from us and the doctors to get the HMO to approve the admission. It's still going to cost tens of thousands of dollars since the center is out of network. This is the third time we've had to do this and our daughter is only 9. How much more of this can we take? When is all this treatment going to make a lasting difference?" (Susan)

"Michelle knows how to play the system. At home, she was a screaming, knife-brandishing demon. At the emergency room, she was a sweet, quiet little angel. It took describing every single, horrifying detail of her behavior during the previous eight hours to get them to take us seriously. I convinced them to call her psychiatrist for confirmation that she really can explode like I was describing. Finally, after talking with the intake counselor at an inpatient care facility, the ER agreed to authorize a 72-hour mental health hold. They arranged for her to be transferred, by ambulance, to the facility, where she spent three hours happily chatting with the counselor. The counselor managed to get the insurance company to authorize a three-day admission. For the first two days, she was as perfect as could be. On the

third day, she exploded. I knew she would finally wear out her ability to control herself and was relieved that it happened while she was still there. After experiencing the full strength of her rage, the facility obtained authorization for a longer stay in the inpatient unit and then a transfer to the residential care unit, where she stayed for several months." (Candelle)

If you do come to the point when you have to hospitalize your child, here are some important things to know in order to manage the situation:

▲ If your location or insurance coverage requires you to go to a regular hospital, it probably won't have a pediatric psychiatric unit. Your child will have to be transferred to another facility to be admitted and treated. If you know where you prefer your child to go, inform the hospital staff and stay very involved as they talk to the insurance company to make sure your child has the best chance of going there.

▲ Many inpatient facilities are open at night. If the crisis comes at night, your child doesn't necessarily have to stay in the emergency room or in a regular hospital waiting for morning to come to get admitted into a psychiatric unit. Make sure the hospital at least attempts to contact the facility to see if your child can be admitted during the night.

"Christian lost it at school. After he got in trouble with his teacher, he kicked the bus and screamed at the principal. My wife picked him up and took him to his therapist. Christian put on the therapist's radio so loud no one could talk, then had a fit when I turned it down. I tried to restrain him, but he kept kicking and punching and cursing. The therapist told him he had a few minutes to try to calm down or she would do an assessment for an intervention for hospitalization. Of course, he wouldn't calm down. He went from anger, to laughter, to spitting to cursing. She called the police to have them take him to the clinic. It took 4 cops to get him there. He even tried to hit them! They finally calmed him down and got him to go. From the clinic, we waited for an ambulance to take him to a psychiatric hospital 4 hours away. Then it took us 3 hours to fill out forms there. We were up all night." (Mark)

▲ If you feel that you can control your child and ensure her safety, you might be able to transfer her from the regular hospital to the psychiatric hospital. If not, she'll be transferred by ambulance.

▲ The idea behind a psychiatric hospital is to provide intense treatment and to ensure your child's safety. Once your child's medications have been adjusted and she's received enough therapy that she is somewhat stable, such as not being an immediate suicide risk or not experiencing severe psychosis, she might need ongoing, long-term care in a residential or day treatment program. The hospital should inform you about their recommendations for continued care and assist you in placing your child in an appropriate treatment program, if necessary.

▲ Once your child is checked into an inpatient treatment program, it's natural to want to ask how long she'll be there, what the treatment will consist of, how often you can visit her, etc. After such intense caregiving, it will seem strange to just turn her over to someone else's care. While you certainly have to get your concerns addressed by the program, they might not be able to give you exact answers until they've had the opportunity to assess your child and begin treatment. You'll have to balance your desire for information with the need to avoid irritating the caregivers. Again, ask your psychiatrist for help. Have him/her get answers, provide professional input and represent you to some degree. If you don't get the answers you need once your child has been assessed, get very vocal with both the psychiatrist and the caregivers. You are still the parent.

▲ In most cases, by the time hospitalization becomes the solution, your child will be feeling so bad or be so out of control that he doesn't really care where he is or what's happening to him. Admitting him to a hospital will probably be much harder on you than on him. On the flip side, though, one or both of you may be so relieved to receive some intense assistance that checking in is a very positive experience. Not only are both extremes okay, but you might fluctuate between them.

▲ While your child is in the hospital, the hospital psychiatrists take over. They should be gathering information from and informing your child's regular psychiatrist, but they are in charge of care during the hospital stay. This is also true if your child goes into a residential treatment program.

▲ Make your schedule as flexible as possible. You will be attending family therapy sessions, having meetings with the staff, and visiting your child.

YOUR FEELINGS DURING A CRISIS

During a real crisis, everyone's attention is focused on the child, as it should be. At some point, though, you're going to have to acknowledge and deal with your feelings about the situation. On top of feeling heartbroken for your poor child, you may feel guilty that you couldn't help your child avoid the crisis, that you didn't handle it right, that you selfishly wish the whole situation would just go away so you could get some peace and quiet, and that you resent having to spend even more money to treat your child. You might feel angry that everything you've already done isn't good enough.

> *"As terrible as I felt about checking Marie into a hospital, I felt even more terrible about how much I enjoyed having some quiet, peaceful time at home with the rest of my family while she was there. It felt good to have someone else be responsible for her, but I was terrified that they wouldn't take as good care of her as I do." (Bernice)*

It's not just okay to have these kinds of feelings—it's perfectly normal. They shouldn't stop you from doing the best you can do to care for your child. They can make your own stress worse, though. The last thing you need is to have something else to worry about. Try to recognize the feelings, do what you can do make them go away, and continue to care for your child while you have them. Then, bring them up with your own therapist or psychiatrist as soon as you can.

> *"I just got a call from my stepfather. He told me that yesterday my 29 year-old brother left his court-ordered inpatient mental health/substance abuse program. He had one month left of his six-month sentence. He went to a hotel and slit his wrist, then called an ambulance. It was just enough to make sure everyone heard his cry for help and to get him put back into the hospital, but it didn't seriously hurt him. I'm happy that he's 'okay,' but I also feel betrayed. I had believed it when he said he was nervous but happy about leaving the program. That doesn't seem like the right reaction to be having;*

it's way too selfish, but that's how I feel. I also feel stupid. I, in my rational mind, had been listening to the words he had been saying for the last few weeks and helping him problem-solve in a logical way. I obviously failed to realize that if his fears and worries about what to do after the program ended were bothering him so much that he was talking about them, they were far more intense than he was expressing. I had actually been thrilled with how good he sounded every time we talked on the phone. He sounded like he was ready, once again, to try to live somewhat independently and to make some kind of life for himself. I think it was wishful thinking, too. I guess he was just too terrified of really being on his own. He found a way to ensure that he would still be part of a program. I certainly don't think he consciously decided to do this—he says he heard voices that he followed—but it seems just calculated enough to a non-Bipolar mind to indicate a real fear of leaving the program that he was devastated about having to go to in the first place. Stupid me. I let my hopes for him get in the way of his reality.

Yet again, just as things seem like they are starting to work out for him, he somehow sabotages it. My father had paid all his fines. Jesse had done all his community service. My mother created an apartment in the basement of her townhouse for him. Together, my parents and stepparents have spent tens of thousands of dollars on Jesse's mental healthcare, legal defenses, and living expenses. He was essentially scott-free after years of dealing with legal worries that were the consequences of manic episodes in a car. Now, in addition to dealing with the logistics of how to provide care for Jesse (assuming the court doesn't just put him in jail), my poor parents have to deal with their own emotions about what's happening to their son. It breaks my heart to think of my sons being disappointed by a mean comment by a friend or having hurt feelings after a sibling argument. I can't imagine what my parents have now experienced several times as their child's emotions are so upset that he would ruin, if not end, his own life. What's more, they have finally realized that the chances of this being the last time are slim. It's going to go on and on and on. None of us can even bear to guess one fraction of the terrible thoughts that must be going on inside Jesse's head. That would be more than any of us could bear.

At least Jesse is getting treatment now. Imagine what problems he would have had if he, his family and the courts didn't understand that everything he's done is related to his mental illness. With earlier detection of his disorder and treatment that began when he was too young to get into serious trouble, maybe he would have avoided a lot of this." (Sheryl)

"It breaks my heart that I'm so devastated about putting Marcus, 11, into a residential treatment program and he's so happy to be going away from home. He is anxious to meet his roommates and for me to drive the 6 hours back and forth from home to bring him all his stuff. When I said goodbye and tried to hug him, Marc just smiled, turned around and walked away before I could touch him." (Jennifer)

"I didn't feel like a very good mother today. I went to visit my 9 year-old daughter in the psychiatric hospital. I didn't feel anything. All the air has been kicked out of me and I just feel deflated and empty." (Heather)

It takes a lot of professionals to take care of one Bipolar child in crisis. It also takes a lot of family members to make decisions, provide information to the professionals, spend time with the child, handle the insurance, take care of the rest of the family, and do everything else that needs to be done. Make sure you aren't the only one doing what needs to be done. You'll become physically as well as emotional exhausted. If you haven't already figured out how to delegate some of the caregiving duties, now is a good time to learn. Then, once everyone is doing what needs to get done, make sure no one is neglecting their own emotional and physical needs. Refusing to think about anything but the child in crisis isn't going to make that crisis go away, but it could contribute to the development of new crises or problems for other family members.

REGROUPING AFTER THE CRISIS

Learning to trust your own judgment again is one of the most important and most difficult aspects of recovering from a child's crisis. Why didn't you notice the problem earlier so you could do something to avoid it? Why didn't you take your child to healthcare professionals who could have helped avoid it? Did you do the right things at the right times to help your child through the crisis? The guilt and questions go on and on.

Then the worrying starts. Will you be able to notice the signals of an impending crisis next time? Will you be able to help your child avoid future crises? Will you ever be able to stop worrying? Will you ever know what's the "right" thing to do? The answer is that yes, you will. If you consciously try to be aware of how the crisis started, review your decisions and evaluate what you wish you'd done differently, and make a plan of action should the problem ever arise again, you'll be able to feel more in control and able to cope with both everyday situations and crises.

While you're in the crisis, though, it's so hard to imagine getting to a point that you can stop feeling as if you're living under a cloud. Little by little, life will calm down. The new normal may be different from the old normal, and you may not ever be completely free of worrying that another crisis will occur, but you and the rest of your family will adapt to whatever the new reality is.

"Since his diagnosis at age 27, my brother has had several crises that are a direct outcome of his Bipolar Disorder, and the alcohol abuse that often is a result, as well as his Borderline Personality Disorder. My family has become experienced in dealing with the court system, the police, credit card companies, psychiatrists, and mental hospital personnel. We've learned how to research treatment programs, track a missing person better than the police can, conspire to make sure someone is always near Jesse, and hide our anger, frustration and fears from Jesse's adoring nephews. We've found that we're able to rotate responsibility so no one gets too stressed and we can get help when we're getting overwhelmed. We've developed a good system for delegating duties that need to be handled to take care of Jesse and each other. My parents and I have realized that I'm the sister, not the parent, so they have to take the lead in dealing with him. They've even overcome years of post-divorce trauma and now work together to help their son. Most importantly, each of us, in our own way, has discovered that we can't afford to indulge in wishful thinking since it intensifies the disappointment each time the next problem arises. With each new crisis, we try to expend less and less emotional energy. We still try to help as much as we can, of course, but we try not to let Jesse's issues take over our lives and get in the way of our happiness with our own spouses and the other children in the family. There's always a part of us that's waiting for Jesse's next crisis and cringing when the phone rings. At the same time, though, we're hoping that it won't ever happen, but we've learned to carry on our lives in the meantime." (Sheryl)

16
Looking to the Future

BEING REALISTIC ABOUT YOUR EXPECTATIONS

When you've been through or are going through hell, it is natural to look for the light at the end of the tunnel. When you're going through it with a Bipolar child, that light can look very dim and far away. You might not even be able to see it at all. If it's this hard to get through each day when your child is still young, how is your family going to get through the years to come?

It's incredibly important for you and your child to believe that she can have a wonderful future. It's equally as important for you not to have rigid expectations about that future. Most parents enjoy visualizing their children becoming increasingly independent and responsible until they are successfully supporting themselves as adults. Their long-term roles as parents will get easier and less time-consuming. You, however, can't quite have that same expectation. Up to now, almost everything you have done to take care of your Bipolar child has been more intense, lasted longer, and seemed more difficult. You probably worry that you are going to be taking care of your Bipolar child for her whole life.

On the other hand, on top of everything that you have to do and think about on a daily basis, you have the very real concern that your child isn't going to make it through puberty, let alone to adulthood. You might find yourself not even wanting to know everything about the long-term ramifications of Bipolar Disorder because the information can feel so dismal. Fortunately, while the statistics on suicide and Bipolar Disorder are grim, the rate of suicide goes down significantly for children who are diagnosed and treated early. Since you are reading this book, you are taking critical steps that will contribute to your child's long-term well-being. He probably will make it, so you'll want to be ready, willing and able to help him as along as he needs it.

As your child transitions through puberty, hormones and normal biological urges will affect him, just as they do any other preteen and teenager. His already difficult-to-control thoughts and behaviors might intensify. What this means for you is that on top of learning how to parent a teenager, you also need to be extra vigilant about notifying the psychiatrist when medication levels don't seem to be working as well or your child has gone through a major growth spurt. It might also mean finding different caregivers who are skilled in working with teens, rather than children. But there is some good news. Children who were properly diagnosed and treated for their childhood-onset Bipolar Disorder are less likely to have substance abuse problems than individuals with adolescent or adult onset forms or whose childhood-onset Bipolar Disorder wasn't diagnosed and treated when they were young.

> *"I just heard a story about a 17 year-old with Bipolar Disorder. She ran off with a 25 year-old man. Her parents tracked her down in Las Vegas. It scares me to death. I just barely feel able to parent my 8 year-old. What am I going to do when she's a teenager?"* (Lisa)

As much as you're trying to teach your child how to control and care for herself so she can live independently as an adult, you probably already realize that it will be even more terrifying not to have your child under your control. It will feel so strange not to know everything that is happening with her. You want her to succeed on her own, but it scares you to think about what could happen to her when she is.

It could also mean that your child will pop in and out of your life, sometimes wanting you to just leave him alone, sometimes wanting you to take care of him as if he's a child. It's better to expect and accept this than to keep hoping that your child will be able to be totally independent as an adult. You can and will be thrilled when he is, but prepared for when he isn't.

No matter how difficult it is to parent your Bipolar child (and even if you have moments now and then when you wish the whole situation would just magically disappear), you hope that you'll be able to parent your child for as long as she needs to be actively parented, even if it's long beyond the normal 18 years. Hopefully, you'll be able to be there for her as long as she needs you.

> ♥ *I think the hardest part of dealing with this illness for me is the way Julie feels about me when she is angry or sad. It feels as if she truly believes that I don't love or care about her. Nothing could be farther from the truth, but I have yet to find a way to convince her of this during those times. She probably has told me she hates me at least a thousand times. The most important thing to me when all is said and done is that she knows in her mind and heart how desperately I love and have always loved her. I hope she realizes that I have tried my best to always do what I thought was the right thing at the time. I wonder sometimes how she will remember her childhood, if she will remember it how it actually was, or if she will remember it through the eyes of illness.*

CREATING A NEW PERSPECTIVE

Even when you've read this whole book, acknowledged the frustrations, unfulfilled hopes and difficulties that will plague your daily life, and somewhat come to grips with the fact that your beloved child has a brain disorder that can be helped, but not cured, you still might find that uncomfortable feelings crop up. They will probably continue to pop into your head now and then. After all, it's heartbreaking to have to read a book to help you live with and love your child. It seems like it should come so naturally, but those of us with Bipolar children know that it isn't that simple. There are times when we not only hate our children's behaviors, but we actually feel like we hate our children. We hate the type of lives we have to live because of our children's disorder. Yet we adore those children. Our feelings are wrapped up in a twisted web of thoughts that are probably as complicated as those that inhabit our children's minds.

Yet what can we do? This is the hand that life has dealt us. We cannot opt out. We cannot ignore it. We can only learn to change our way of looking at the situation, just as cognitive behavioral therapy will help our children learn to identify, understand and modify their misperceptions.

Who's to say what parenthood is supposed to be like? How do we know that our children won't be the next great artists, philosophers, or writers of the century? Maybe there is an unforeseeable reason why we were chosen to raise these intense, wonderful, special and emotional children. There must be a purpose to the incredible challenge we face.

> *"I've always said that it was a good thing that God gave my daughter to me rather than some of the other parents I've seen. She certainly would have ended up one of those abused children living on the street had she been born to anyone with one ounce less of patience!"* (Emily)

> ♥ *Columbine High School is only a few miles away from where we live, but I don't think it's only its location that makes it feel so "close to home." I have just been devastated by what happened. It definitely brought out some very deep fears from inside. Fears about Julie's future plague me. I certainly don't think Julie could become a mass murderer, but I do worry about what her impulse control, temper and lack of conscience will look like when she is older. There are many times I feel sheer terror about Julie's future. There are as many other times when I feel sure that she is destined for greatness.*

When you're finished mourning what could have been if your child had been born without Bipolar Disorder, you can have the clarity of vision to see what your child really is—a wonderfully complex bundle of energy and emotion who is capable of amazing things. It will take more parental support, more medical support and more personal commitment on his part than it would for a child without a mental illness, but many mentally ill people can and have been successful, productive, and happy members of society.

> ♥ *I learned something really amazing today. I was sitting in a meeting with my daughter's teachers, talking about Julie's progress and struggles. We weren't focusing on her math skills, handwriting, or reading comprehension. We were talking about how many times she was smiling in a day, happy about the fact she was gabbing and giggling with the other kids during class, and glad that she was doing "grade level" work. I realized what was really important. I realized that I needed to use a different ruler to measure her success than I might for another child—or for the child I thought*

I had, or the child I thought she could or should be. I feel as if I had to actually mourn that child I created in my mind and all the potential I gave her for the things that I thought were important. Once I pulled out my new ruler, I realized how much she really was succeeding and how well she was doing on the things others may just take for granted—like being happy. We just assume that when their basic needs are being met, children are happy. I know now, for my child, happiness is our life's goal and is something to savor and appreciate and strive for. Once we can get past what we thought our children would be, we can truly celebrate who they really are.

There truly are many things to actually envy about our lives and our children. Parents of Bipolar children don't take things for granted. No step is ordinary to us. We are moved beyond words by a simple "I love you" from our child. Soccer games, birthday parties, and dance lessons do not bog us down. Instead we spend every day concentrating on being healthy and happy.

Conclusion

As you've been reading about how to parent your own Bipolar child, you've read a lot about the difficulties that Julie, Jesse and Joey have faced. Now we're happy to report on their progress.

> ♥ *I cannot begin to describe the past two weeks. Julie has been doing so incredibly well. We have been doing "real family" things like going to movies and out to dinner. It's been so wonderful having positive experiences with her. I decided this is what it must be like for other families. I'm savoring every minute because I know it can change at any time. I don't remember feeling this "normal" for the last 11 years. Is it possible this nightmare could be over? Intellectually, I know it is not likely—but I still find myself wishing.*

Julie has been relatively stable for the past year, even through the divorce of her parents and the move to a new house. She is attending a private school that specializes in teaching kids with learning differences. Her grades are good, she is happy about going to school, and she has friends that she plays with at school and at home. She takes Concerta, Wellbutrin, Zyprexa, Ritalin, and Tegretol. The only major challenge that she is facing right now is that her growth has slowed. After numerous difficult tests, no reason has been found. We're thrilled that nothing identifiable is wrong, but worried that some of the psychiatric medications may have affected her growth.

Jesse completed a 5 month-long residential treatment program that seems to have given him the tools he needs to manage his own care and be responsible for his own life. He has regular appointments with his therapist and psychiatrist and is taking Neurontin, Lamectal, Zyprexa, Respirdal and Cogentin. It's still a challenge to figure out the right combination, dosage, and times to take his meds to keep him from having side effects like extreme tiredness, acne and weight gain. While he still experiences frequent mood swings, they don't seem to be affecting his lifestyle or behavior. He moved away from home and works for a government agency.

Joey is thrilled that the "happy part" of his brain is bigger and stronger. The "devil" part of his brain is now very, very quiet and hardly ever tells him to do bad things. The "angel" part of his brain sometimes even tells the "devil" to shut up! He has stopped his repetitive finger licking and frequent trips to the bathroom. He says he doesn't worry about things like the walls of his room falling down, a bridge collapsing on the car, or the car running out of gas anymore. In fact, he has a hard time remembering that he ever did. His attention span at school seems better and he doesn't talk constantly anymore. He's happy that his Serzone pills have helped him. He is excited that his cognitive-behavioral therapy has gone well and his medication dosage is being reduced.

Even though things are going well at this point, there are still many unanswered questions and unspoken fears. There is no way to know exactly what the future will bring. How will our mentally ill children react when their hormones start raging? How will they handle the presence of drugs, alcohol and violence in middle and high school? Will puberty bring on new symptoms and reactions to medications? Of course, no parent knows how his/her child will handle the difficult teen years. Parents can't expect their vision of their child as a grown up to be fully realized. In many ways, we are in the same boat as everyone else as we think about our children's futures – we just have many more variables to deal with.

Our own sense of responsibility may be stronger, too. We not only have to learn how to parent teenagers, but we have to prepare ourselves to parent for many years afterwards, if necessary. We not only have to look for signs of inappropriate friends and substance abuse, but also figure out how to deal with a rebellious child who might want to replace prescription meds with illegal drugs. Our understanding that our children need to develop their independence may be overshadowed by our fears about them being less supervised. As usual, our parenting experiences will just be more intense and more complicated than other parents'.

No matter what happens, though, we will go on loving our children, doing the best we can do. As you know, no guarantee comes with the beautiful baby that was put in your arms. No parent ever knows that their child is going to be perfect, happy, and safe at all times. But we can just love them, support them as much as possible, take care of ourselves while we care for our children, and find joy and hope from the many wonderful aspects of our lives and the lives of our Bipolar children.

Glossary

TERMS RELATED TO THE DIAGNOSIS AND TREATMENT OF BIPOLAR DISORDER

Following are definitions of some terms that are used in this book or may be used by your mental healthcare professional when diagnosing and treating your child.

Behavior Plan: An organized program that parents and mental healthcare professionals develop together for parents to use consistent and appropriate parenting techniques to help a child improve his behavior.

Cognitive: Relating to thinking, awareness, knowledge, and reasoning.

Cognitive Behavioral Therapy: Therapy that focuses on actual current situations and problems and addresses thoughts, feeling and actions and how they affect each other.

Colic: A term used to describe severe irritability and prolonged crying in infants.

Comorbidity: The tendency of different disorders to occur together in the same person.

Contraindication: A reason why a certain medication shouldn't be given; for example, a previous allergic reaction to the medication.

Cycling: Fluctuating between periods of mania and depression.

Day Treatment: An outpatient treatment program, typically including school, that children attend regularly, usually every weekday.

Delusion: A false belief that is held even though there is evidence that it is false.

Depression: A condition characterized by an inability to concentrate, sleep disturbances, feelings of extreme sadness, dejection and helplessness.

Diagnosis: A term given by a professional to describe a set of particular symptoms.

Disorder: An atypical condition that affects the function of mind or body.

Dysphoria: An emotional state characterized by depression and mania that either co-occur or alternate back and forth quickly and frequently.

Generic: Refers to a medication's chemical name, which is not protected by a trademark and, therefore, can be used by any manufacturers of the medication.

Hallucination: A false or distorted sensory perception of events or objects that seems very real. The person may or may not know they are having a hallucination. There are many types of hallucinations:

▲ Auditory—perception of sound. For example, hearing voices or holding imaginary conversations with another person.

▲ Gustatory—perception of taste. For example, incorrectly perceiving that food tastes extremely bad.

▲ Olfactory—perception of odor. For example, smelling intense smoke even though no one else smells it.

▲ Somatic—perception of experiences affecting the body. For example, feeling like electricity is running through the skin.

▲ Tactile—perception of touch. For example, feeling of being touched or something crawling on the skin.

▲ Visual—involving sight. For example, seeing things that are not really there or extreme distortions of what is there.

Hyperactivity: Abnormally increased activity.

Inpatient Facility: A treatment program that admits the patient into a hospital-type setting for 24-hour per day care and treatment.

Malaise: An overall feeling of discomfort, uneasiness, and/or being unwell.

Manic/Mania: A period of having many rapidly changing ideas, extreme physical activity, fast talking and inappropriately intense enthusiasm.

Manic Depression: What Bipolar Disorder used to be called.

Mood Disorder: A condition marked by abnormally intense and extreme moods.

Neurotypical: Normal mental functions related to moods, thoughts, and perceptions.

Neurodevelopmental: Related to the development of mental functions, such as moods, thoughts, and perceptions.

NOS: A catch-all category that means "Not Otherwise Specified" and is used along with a diagnosis when symptoms don't exactly match the description for that particular disorder.

Parity: The requirement that two different things be treated equally. In this case, insurance companies must provide parity in coverage for biologically-based mental disorders and all other types of physical illnesses.

Pediatrician: A medical doctor who monitors your child's physical health, may supervise some of the medical tests required for monitoring certain psychiatric medications, and coordinates the full "health" care for your child.

Pharmacist: A medical professional who prepares and dispenses medications and has extensive knowledge of the effects and side effects of medications, their interactions with other drugs, and dosages.

Precocious: Unusually early development or maturity, especially in cognitive abilities.

Provisional Diagnosis: How a mental healthcare professional characterizes a diagnosis that he/she thinks is accurate, but has not yet been fully proven.

Psychiatrist: A medical doctor who can prescribe medications and provide therapy or other treatment and may supervise some of the medical tests required to monitor certain psychiatric medications.

Psychologist: A professional, who is not a medical doctor, who can provide psychological testing, identify learning disorders, diagnose mental disorders, and provide therapeutic treatment, but cannot prescribe medication.

Psychosis: An emotional state characterized by a deranged personality style, loss of touch with reality, and loss of normal social functioning.

Rage: An intense, explosive, prolonged and violent fit of anger.

Residential Care: A facility where patients live for the duration of their treatment.

Sensory: Relating to the senses (smell, touch, taste, hearing, and sight).

Separation Anxiety: Extreme distress that a child feels when separated from a parent.

Social Worker: A licensed, trained professional who can coordinate treatment and provide therapy, assessment, and referrals.

Suspension: A form of dispensing medication where the drug is crushed and the particles are mixed into a liquid but are not dissolved. A pharmacist may be able to make a suspension for your child when a liquid form of the medication is not available from the manufacturer.

Tardive Dsykenesia: Slow, involuntary movements, often of the tongue, lips or arms, that are a possible and serious side effect of some psychiatric medications.

Therapist: A non-medical professional who has training in therapy, but isn't licensed as a psychologist. These professionals may be social workers or individuals who obtained a degree or certification related to psychology.

Tricotillomania: A psychological disorder characterized by the recurrent pulling out of one's hair for pleasure or relief, resulting in noticeable hair loss.

Additional Resources

Insurance and Other Social Service Program Information

▲ U.S. Dept. of Health and Human Services (health insurance programs for uninsured kids)... 877-KIDS-NOW ....www.insurekidsnow.gov

▲ Supplemental Security Income information www.ssa.gov/disability

▲ Association of Maternal and Child Health Programs ...202-775-0436

▲ National Association of Insurance Commissioners 202-624-7790

Online Resources on Bipolar Disorder

Each of the following websites provides mental health information, Bipolar Disorder information, resources, support, and/or printed materials for order. We've chosen to provide a sample of websites that are sponsored by formal organizations. There are many other helpful websites available, many of which are sponsored by individuals with direct experience of Bipolar Disorder. Just surf the web using the keyword "Bipolar." You'll be amazed at how much you can find.

▲ National Institute of Mental Health 800-411-1222
....www.nimh.nih.gov

▲ The National Alliance for the Mentally Ill 800-950-NAMI
....www.nami.org

▲ Juvenile Bipolar Research Foundation 203-222-7179
...............................www.bpchildresearch.org

▲ Child and Adolescent Bipolar Foundation 847-256-8525
. . . . .www.bpkids.org

▲ Bipolor Disorder Information Center 800-933-2632
. . . . .www.mhsource.com

▲ National Depressive & Manic-Depressive Association . . .800-826-3632
. . . . .www.ndmda.org

▲ Depressive & Related Affective Disorders Association . . .410-955-4647
. . . . .www.med.jhu.drada

▲ American Psychiatric Association .202-682-6000
. . . . .www.psych.org

▲ American Psychological Association 800-964-2000
. . . . .www.helping.apa.org

▲ National Information Center for Children & Youth With Disabilities
(800-695-0285) . . . . .www.nichcy.org

▲ American Academy of Child & Adolescent Psychiatry . . .202-966-7300
. . . . .www.aacap.org

▲ Knowledge Exchange Network 800-789-2647
. . . . .www.mentalhealth.org

▲ Johns Hopkins University . . . . .www.med.jhu.edu/Bipolar

▲ Mayo Clinic . . . . .www.mayohealth.org

▲ Stanford University . . . . .www.stanford.edu

Hot Lines/Help Lines

▲ National Suicide Prevention Hot Line 800-999-9999

▲ National Alliance for the Mentally Ill Help Line (info and referrals) . . .
. . . . .800-950-NAMI

Other Books On Bipolar Disorder and its Treatment

▲ *The Bipolar Child: The Definitive and Reassuring Guide to Childhood's Most Misunderstood Disorder* by Demitri Papolos, M.D. and Janice Papolos

▲ *Bipolar Disorders: A Guide to Helping Children and Adolescents* by Mitzi Waltz

▲ *Straight Talk about Psychiatric Medications for Kids* by Timothy E. Wilens, MD

Index

More from Perspective Publishing

Perspective Publishing is a small independent publishing company which helps parents with the problems you face every day: discipline, friendship problems, talking with your kids, balancing work and family, challenging and inspiring your kids.

   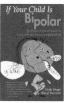  

Good Friends Are Hard to Find: Help your child find, make and keep friends by Fred Frankel, Ph.D.   Step-by-step, parents learn to help their 5 to 12-year-olds make friends and solve problems with other kids, including teasing, bullying and meanness. Based on UCLA's world renowned Children's Social Skills Program, this book teaches clinically tested techniques that really work.   ISBN: 0-9622036-7-X, paperback. 6"x9"; 242 pages; $13.95

Win the Whining War & Other Skirmishes: A family peace plan by Cynthia Whitham, MSW   This easy-to-use guide helps parents increase cooperation and reduce conflict with children ages 2-12. Step-by-step, parents learn how to cut out all the annoying behavior (tantrums, teasing, dawdling, interrupting, complaining, etc.) that drives them crazy.   ISBN: 0-9622036-3-7, paperback. 6"x9"; 208 pages; $13.95

Also available in Spanish:
Gana la Guerra de los Berrinches y Otras Contiendas: Un plan de paz familiar
        ISBN: 1-930085-04-4; paperback, 6"x9"; 208 pages; $13.95

"The Answer is NO": Saying it and sticking to it by Cynthia Whitham, MSW
Tackling twenty-six situations that plague parents of 2 to 12-year-olds, this book helps parents define their values, build good parenting habits, and set firm, fair limits. Bedtime, pets, makeup, music, TV, homework, and designer clothes are just a few of the problems covered.
        ISBN: 0-9622036-4-5, paperback. 6"x9"; 224 pages; $13.95l

If Your Child is Bipolar: The Parent-to-Parent Guide to Living with and Loving a Bipolar Child by Cindy Singer and Sheryl Gurrentz   This supportive guide helps parents deal with the everyday challenges of parenting a child with a psychiatric disorder. From getting homework done to interacting with siblings to getting ready to go to a doctors appointment, this book helps parents feel more in control of the situation and more positive towards their child.
        ISBN: 1-930085-06-0; paperback, 6"x9"; 221 pages; $18.95

The Guilt-Free Guide to Your New Life as a Mom: Practical ways to take care of yourself, your life & your baby – all the the same time by Sheryl Gurrentz
Expectant and new moms need help with everything, and this easy-to-use practical book helps new mothers take care of themselves and everything else in their lives while taking care of their babies.   ISBN: 1-930085-01-X; paperback, 6"x9"; 250 pages; $14.95

Before She Gets Her Period:Talking to your daughter about menstruation by Jessica B. Gillooly, Ph.D.   This friendly book has up-to-date information and uses real personal stories, exercises and activities to help parents talk with their daughters about menstruation — even if their daughters don't want to talk. It's the only book about menstruation written for parents.
        ISBN: 0-9622036-9-6, paperback. 6"x9"; 166 pages; $13.95

(more on other side)
Order now: 1-800-330-5851 or www.familyhelp.com

More from Perspective Publishing

AMERICA'S DAUGHTERS: 400 Years of American Women by Judith Head
This easy-to-read yet carefully researched history of American women from the 1600s to today is illustrated with 150 photos and period drawings, and gives children and adults both an overview of what life was like for women, and profiles of more than 50 individual women, both famous and not so well known.   ISBN: 0-9622036-8-8 Paperback. 8"x10"; 136 pages; $16.95

The Invasion of Planet Wampetter by Samuel H. Pillsbury illustrated by Matthew Angorn
Pudgy orange young wampetters Eloise and Gartrude Tub save their planet from becoming an intergalactic tourist trap in this non-violent and funny space adventure. As entertaining for grown-ups as for kids, it is a perfect family read aloud.

> ISBN: 0-9622036-6-1, hardcover. 6"x9"; 144 pages; $15.00
> ISBN: 1-930085-05-2; paperback.6"x9"; 144 pages; $8.95

Mission to California by Samuel H. Pillsbury illustrated by David Kantrowitz
It's another wampetter adventure and this time the Tub family is off to Californiato recover the sacred Book of Jokes, overcoming family conflicts, rampaging elehants, a sneaky professor, and a ferocious California legal system.   ISBN: 1-930085-03-6; paperback. 6"x9"; 140 pages; $8.95

The Summer Camp Handbook: Everything you need to find, choose and get ready for overnight camp—and skip the homesickness by Christopher A. Thurber, PhD and Jon C. Malinowski. PhD   This practical book guides parents step-by-step through the entire process of choosing and sending children to overnight camp. It also includes extensive resource listings.

> ISBN: 1-930085-00-1; paperback. 6"x9"; 250 pages; $14.95

Better Than Take-Out (& Faster, Too): Quick and easy cooking for busy families by Pamela Marx   Even the busiest families can enjoy homemade meals with these fast, easy and delicious dinners. The book is full of dozens of time-saving tips, and the recipes are so good you can serve them to company.   ISBN: 1-930085-02-8; paperback. 6"x9"; 160 pages; $14.95

Survival Tips for Working Moms: 297 REAL Tips from REAL Moms by Linda Goodman Pillsbury   This light but no-nonsense practical resource can help every working mom. From chores to childcare, errands to exercise, this book makes life easier.

> ISBN: 0-9622036-5-3, paperback. 6"x9"; 192 pages; $10.95

ORDER FORM

Qty/Title	Price/@	Total
Subtotal		——
Tax (CA residents 8.25%)		——
Shipping ($4 for 1st , $1 for @ add'l)		——
TOTAL ENCLOSED		——

Name:_____

Organization: _____

Address:_____

City, State, Zip:_____

Phone:_____

Credit Card #:_____

Exp. Date: _____

Signature:_____

PERSPECTIVE
PUBLISHING

Send to: Perspective Publishing, Inc.
2528 Sleepy Hollow Dr. #A • Glendale, CA 91206
Or call: 1-800-330-5851
Or order on the internet: www.familyhelp.com